C L A S S R O O M   A S S E S S M E N T

What's Working in High Schools?
Book One

C L A S S R O O M   A S S E S S M E N T

What's Working in High Schools?

Book One

Edited by:

Anne Davies, Ph.D. & Kathy Busick, Ph.D.

Connections
Publishing

Cover Art and Book Design: START Communications (info@startcreative.ca)
Cover Photo: www.free-pictures-photos.com
Editing: Annie Jack (beachwalker@shaw.ca)
Project Management: Judith Hall-Patch

Notes to Readers:

- All royalties go to the International Assessment Consortium to further the positive impact of assessment *for* learning.

- This book is printed using environmentally friendly ink and recycled paper.

- Canadian/British and US spelling is used throughout these two volumes, according to the country of origin of the authors.

Library and Archives Canada Cataloguing in Publication
Classroom Assessment : What's Working in High Schools / Edited by Anne Davies and Kathy Busick.
Includes bibliographical references.
ISBN 978-0-9736352-9-4
1. Educational tests and measurements. 2. Education, Secondary.
I. Davies, Anne, 1955- II. Busick, Kathy, 1942
LB3051.C53 2007   371.26   C2007-903648-1

Contents

Prologue

The Belted Kingfisher is a common waterside resident in British Columbia. It is often seen hovering above, peering down and examining its target before plunging headfirst into the water. The Kingfisher series is sponsored by the group of educators who have gathered annually since 2000 for a week of intense learning and reflection, using assessment *for* learning practices. These lead learners come together to rise above and reflect on their work, to survey the challenges they face in their daily practice, and to focus on their goal of more effectively supporting learners. Then they leave to plunge, once again, into their chosen work. This book invites you to peer through the eyes of high school educators and take the plunge into assessment *for* learning.

Meeting the challenges that arise from the classroom assessment research findings – particularly implementing assessment *for* learning – is not an easy task. High schools are decidedly demanding environments without the additional challenge of learning and developing a new teaching practice. However, the educators who have contributed to this two-volume set are convinced that the effort is well worthwhile. Their examples will demonstrate how assessment *for* learning techniques can actually make the educator's job easier and more effective, for both students and teachers.

Our intention is to inform and support high school teachers and those who support high school teachers in their work, as they engage in learning about what is working and what might need to change so that classroom assessment practices directly support student learning. The authors of these chapters come from a variety of disciplines – English, World Languages, Social Studies, Mathematics, Science, Creative Writing, Philosophy, Alternative Education, Fine Arts, Journalism and Media – because we know that while some assessment practices are similar across disciplines, there are also variations of practices that are unique to different disciplines.

Each author writes from his or her personal experience and perspective—sharing struggles, concrete examples and hard-won insights. Some have many years of experience, others are in the early stages of their professional life. All are learning, themselves, as their students succeed. Together, their voices affirm the power of classroom assessment to increase learning across different disciplines and school systems. They provide a rainbow of strategies and pathways for teaching and learning success. As you read, reflect on your own assessment practices. Identify ideas or refinements that might support you and your students. Black line masters are included at the end of each book to help you adapt and incorporate these ideas into your individual situations.

While it is true that quality classroom assessment takes time to learn to do well, research, and teachers themselves, tell us that the time is worth taking in terms of student engagement, motivation, learning, and achievement. In *Classroom Assessment: What's Working in High Schools,* high school teachers share what's working for them as they implement quality classroom assessment in their classrooms and schools. In addition, this rich collection of practical classroom assessment ideas is complemented by the expertise of knowledgeable professionals who work in support of classroom teachers and student learning. We thank all the authors for their willingness to share their learning.

Books One and Two describe a complete classroom assessment process that sees teachers in a wide variety of teaching contexts and subject area disciplines engaging in classroom assessment that works. As you read, notice teachers beginning with the end in mind, thinking through evidence or proof of learning, and considering what quality work looks like. Notice students being engaged in the process of understanding the learning destination, considering the evidence they can collect, and beginning to learn. See how teachers directly involve students in co-constructing criteria, self-assessing in relation to criteria, giving themselves and others specific, descriptive feedback, applying feedback to improve their work, collecting evidence or proof of their ongoing learning, and then, summarizing what they have learned to present proof of learning to teachers, parents and others. Lastly, hear teachers describe how they use their criteria-based professional judgment to summarize the achievement of students, so they can report using required report card symbols. As these chapters illustrate, quality classroom assessment is a dynamic process involving students and teachers.

Classroom assessment takes place within a context that is increasingly regulated. In this book, high school teachers from across Canada and the United States are renovating their classroom assessment practices to align with research which confirms and describes practices that improve learning. Day-by-day, they work to address local and state/provincial learning mandates and comply with multiplying regulations. Within this pressurized work environment, these teachers are challenging themselves to grow along with their students. They are going the extra mile, using classroom assessment to identify their students' strengths and learning needs, and applying those insights to adjust their own teaching – thus, increasing the learning for all.

This book is dedicated to all the students and teachers with whom we learn.

Theme One:
Beginning with Students

Theme One:
Beginning with Students

Quality classroom assessment begins with teachers studying the standards or learning outcomes for which they, and their students, are responsible, so that they can prepare with the end in mind. They take a look at where their students are in relation to the learning outcomes, asking: What strengths do my students come with? and What do they need in order to reach the learning outcomes? Teachers consider possible evidence or proof of learning, as well as grade level expectations for quality. Then they work to engage students in the process of building a learning community, coming to understand the learning destination for the subject or course, thinking through what success might look like, and planning to collect the kind of evidence of learning they will need to show others.

1   In the first chapter, **Drew Pisani**, an English teacher from Maine, relates how he involves students in developing classroom agreements which become criteria for everyday and semester expectations. He also describes how he has used assessment *for* learning to engage and motivate students to take a very active role in their learning, as well as in his own learning as he designed a creative writing course.

2   **Philip Divinsky**, a vocational teacher, and **Thomas Lafavore**, Director of Educational Planning for Portland (Maine) Public Schools, write about involving students with special needs in developing a community of learners in an alternative high school program. By building classroom agreements, teacher and students create a safe and collaborative environment in which learners can take risks, receive productive feedback and believe themselves capable of learning and producing quality work.

3   **Stephanie Doane,** a teacher of humanities in Maine, uses assessment practices to support lifelong learning in her Social Studies classes. She describes how her students produce proof of learning using progress folios, student-involved conferences and student-set criteria, and how she provides descriptive feedback as well as time for students to be reflective, even in an environment of increased testing and reporting in percentage grades.

4   **Alice Yates** illustrates how she uses assessment *for* learning practices in a Modern Language course to involve students and help them learn. She documents her successes with a multi-level class in her New England high school.

5   Concluding this theme, **Rick Stiggins**, Executive Director of the ETS Assessment Training Institute in Portland, Oregon, affirms the work of these classroom teachers as he discusses the importance of assessment *for* learning as a vehicle for motivating and engaging learners. He writes, "If a student decides that the learning is beyond reach for her or him or that the risk of public failure is too great and too humiliating, then regardless of what we adults do, there will be no learning (page 42)."

Drew Pisani

Drew Pisani, B.A., M.A., has taught English for over five years at Deering High School in Portland, Maine. He has been an integral member of the assessment team collaborating with interdisciplinary colleagues at both Deering and Yarmouth High School. He has presented his assessment practices at conferences and continues to modify them with the help of his new students.

Assessing the Unassessable
by Drew Pisani

So much of what our students do well to demonstrate their conceptual understandings is not easily measurable. For instance, a student who demonstrates his insights and understanding through excellent classroom participation may not show the same degree of understanding on a written test or other assessment. In addition, a writer of poetry may exhibit brilliant clarity, rich language, and powerful voice that she cannot possibly achieve in a thesis paper. Students can and should show their learning in a variety of ways; teachers must open doors for students to be successful. But how do we assess such intangibles as participation and poetry? How can we give verbal and written feedback, as well as a grade, on something so abstract? There are no clear-cut answers to these questions, but there are several ways in which we can help our students understand what quality participation and poetry look like, and how to achieve both.

Creating The Mission Statement

Initially, teachers must work with students (and students with teachers) to establish criteria concerning quality work. The first full day of any class can best be spent creating guidelines for classroom behavior, work habits, and expectations. This establishes an early community, as students and teachers share a vision that persists for the duration of the course.

In small groups, students generate wish lists of the ideal way they want everyone in class to function. I compile these lists into a master, add a few of my own (and eliminate far-fetched fantasies like "no homework"), and then, together, students and I narrow the list to a few highlights that include almost all of the ideas presented. As easily as that, students have created criteria with teacher guidance regarding the everyday and semester expectations. Student criteria are focused on, but not limited to, daily behavior and work ethic, whereas teacher expectations include being available for extra help, providing a judgment-free zone, giving praise often, and being open-minded. Together we build and refine the criteria and then formulate a sentence that becomes the class's mission statement.

Here's a sample mission statement from my creative writing class:

> We, the Creative Writing Class in 203, agree to show respect and encouragement for everyone and reserve judgments. We will be punctual to class and with work, collaborative, relaxed, involved and focused, resourceful, and prepared. We will express feelings, get right to it, check emotions at the door, show unlimited creative flow, and achieve success in our writing and lives.

Every member of the class, including the teacher, signs the mission statement. Then it is posted in the front of the room. If anyone veers from this class-generated set of guidelines, I remind him or her that by signing the mission statement, he or she agreed to these behaviors. The mission statement serves well as a reminder of daily classroom expectations and has proven to be a substantial improvement in parent communication when displayed both at open house and on teacher websites. As a result, we clearly define abstract classroom expectations, and students believe in and adhere to them since they helped to create them.

"My students and I determine what the components of their overall semester grade should be."

Once the mission statement has been signed and posted, the class can now exist and function as a community of learners. This also serves as a comfortable introduction to setting criteria with these students, a process which will occur more frequently. For example, on the first day of all my courses, my students and I determine what the components or categories of their overall semester grade should be, and how each should be weighted. Then we begin narrowly defining each to make the expectations as clear as possible, beginning with classroom participation.

Developing Classroom Participation Criteria

Depending on the class, participation may have a huge or minimal impact on a student's overall grade. Classroom participation and work habits are often evaluated differently from class to class in the same school; there is no right or wrong way to assess this intangible, but teachers must be clear with expectations and a shared vision with all students, acknowledging what excellent participation looks like.

How then can you assess class participation? Well, you don't; you let the students assess themselves based on criteria established by the class. Once again you take the time, about fifteen minutes, for the students to collaborate in small groups or as a class, to determine what are the most important facets of classroom participation. Some may include showing respect, listening well, contributing often, having insightful input, and so on. Then you can modify the list with student support. (This is important; make sure they agree with you so you're not forcing your ideas onto them.) The list of criteria becomes the foundation for a rubric.

Once you have your rubric categories (criteria), then you must take the time with your class to discuss with them what each level looks and sounds like and to model it with your students so they know your expectations and how to effectively assess their own participation. Students can also be involved in establishing a scale for different levels of each category, such as numeric values (1-4) or evaluative terms (exceeds, meets, partially meets, doesn't meet). As students become confident about participation criteria, examples of great participation will emerge; it is always amazing and powerful when a quiet student suddenly offers insightful input that changes a teacher's way of thinking. I remember when a normally subdued student of mine brilliantly interpreted the words "Roger" and "Over and Out" in Tim O'Brien's story, *Speaking of Courage,* to represent a flashback to the fighting in Vietnam by a soldier who was trying to readjust to post-war America. This and other models can serve as teaching moments throughout the semester, as a way of helping struggling students to gain the confidence and ability to participate more often and more insightfully.

Figure 1 ▼

Class Participation Self-Evaluation

As our educational journey for the semester is approaching a close, I would like you to reflect on your contributions to the class as a whole. Ask yourself these questions. Did you help others learn more? Did you help broaden the classroom discussions? Were you actively involved and engaged most of the time? Based on the questions below, please assess your participation in Junior Honors English. Be honest with yourself, your peers, and your teacher. Then convert your score to a grade. Use the scale below to rank the questions.

1 = never	2 = sometimes	3 = most of the time	4 = all of the time

1. I participate daily in DOL (grammar) by contributing a correction. _____ (1-4)

2. I often raise my hand in class in an attempt to answer or ask a question. _____ (1-4)

3. I help other students during group work and text-based quizzes. _____ (1-4)

4. I respect my peers by not talking over them and waiting for them to finish before I respond. I respect my peers' opinions and willingness to take risks. _____ (1-4)

5. I am not afraid to think outside the box and offer different interpretations or ideas. I am not afraid to take risks. I support my opinions and ideas with evidence. _____ (1-4)

6. I have been present in and punctual to class this past quarter. _____ (1-4)

7. I have utilized my class time effectively for English class. _____ (1-4)

8. In have utilized my computer lab / class time effectively in class. _____ (1-4)

9. I offer insightful interpretations in class. _____ (1-4)

Grading Scale – Average the scores above (add them and divide the total by nine)

2	2.1	2.2	2.3	2.4	2.5	2.6	2.7	2.8	2.9	3.0	3.1	3.2	3.3	3.4	3.5	3.6	3.7	3.8	3.9	4.0
70	72	74	76	77	78	79	81	83	84	85	86	87	89	91	93	94	95	96	98	100

Some students may have difficulty assessing their own participation; therefore, have them assess not only themselves but also a partner they can observe for a week or two. The participation rubric can be used for the entire semester or modified by the class at any point. Certain categories such as respect and attendance may remain constant, but others, such as quality and quantity of contributions, may change depending on the level of the class and different student and leader expectations.

The rubric can also be used any number of times throughout the term to assess student participation and as a constant reminder for reluctant participants. A student's class participation grade becomes a combination of these self-assessments and is no longer a teacher's subjective mark. Therefore, both students and their parents will tend to accept the participation grades since the criteria have been established by the class are clear, measurable, and attainable.

Teaching and Assessing Creative Writing

"I committed my first error by using another teacher's rubric…"

Since my first day of teaching high school English, I longed for the opportunity to teach creative writing as a semester-long elective so I could savor this pathway to enlightenment with my students on their inward journey to the self. In my mind I created several awe-inspiringly flawless activities destined to produce writing prowess. After years of waiting, my time arrived. Although elated at first, trepidations quickly emerged like dust bunnies from beneath the couch. Too many questions lingered. How can I teach creativity? What are my students expecting of me? How am I going to assess student creative writing?

After some internal and external dialogue, I approached my department head and asked to be reassigned. I no longer wanted my dream class, a course now fraught with too many unknowns and uncertainties. When I was told that I had to do it, I hounded every experienced writing teacher in the building for advice. I purchased books with writing advice and exercises and photocopied multiple handouts as I searched for the answers to my profound questions.

The answers came not from any book or teacher but from my students themselves. They too approached class anxiously, worried about workload, expectations, teacher attitude, and other unknowns. They too were wondering how I, an unpublished writer, would be helping them to become excellent writers. Spending the first day of class creating a mission statement, we broke down barriers, had fun, and knew where everybody stood.

By establishing classroom criteria, we paved the way for creating writing rubrics together. We were speaking the same language and acknowledging each other's needs. They were vividly aware of every expectation of them and where I stood on every issue from assessment to tardiness, and I was immediately in sync with their needs.

We began the semester by writing memoirs, and I committed my first error by using another teacher's rubric for assessing them. I was assessing based on someone else's criteria and standards, not my own, and my students had no part in creating them. This was mostly out of laziness and my continued quest to prepare this class as quickly as possible for their arduous journey toward literary greatness. I immediately noticed student apathy toward the assignment; the writing was a struggle without any enthusiasm for the piece. As a result, I decided not to skip the process of building criteria the next time.

As we progressed into a short story unit, we all became (or had to become) proficient editors. With a class of twenty-four, it was nearly impossible for me to assess both rough and final drafts for every major piece of writing. So, after reading several excellent short stories by Hemingway, Atwood, and other superb writers, the class generated a list of criteria that should be present in a great story (Figure 2a). With my assistance, this became a rubric for their stories, which each student used as a peer-editing sheet to assess two other students' stories. Each student had to find three examples of evidence for showing details of place, character, and action. The initial rubric is shown in Figure 2b.

Figure 2a ▼

Check the column that applies to the category.

	Excellent	Good	Average	Poor
Showing details		✔		3
Organization (effective beginning and ending)		✔		3
Cohesion			✔	2
Voice			✔	3
Sense of character, action, and place		✔		3
Word choice			✔	3
Grammar		✔		3

Comment on any of those categories. $20/7 = 2.9 = 87$

Also suggest ways of improving this piece...

Figure 2b ▼

Proofreading Exercise for Creative Writing

As peer editors, each of you will peruse (read carefully) at least two students' works and identify aspects of each according to the chart below. It is vital to provide constructive criticism, or warm and cool feedback. Don't simply say, "Nice job!" and draw a little smiley face. Become both teacher and critic, and through this you will improve your writing. You must use the constructive criticism of your peers to improve your piece; if you're unsure about it, see me.

Place: Identify three showing details that take you to this place.

1. "The inside of the fridge smelled even worse; moldy cheese, week-old Chinese food, sour milk, rotten eggs, wilted lettuce."
2. "I was sitting in my old brown leather chair…"
3. "It sounded like whatever was happening was happening right outside my three-story apartment building."

Character: Identify three showing details that help you experience who these characters are.

1. "I was sitting on my old brown leather chair staring at the clock on my microwave, engrossed in deep thoughts…"
2. He's an ex hit man.
3. "Blood's a pain in the ass to clean up, I thought to myself."

Action: Identify three showing details that help you to see or perceive the action.

1. "I was running down a set of metal fire escape stairs and I slipped and sliced my shin along one of the sharp edges of a stair."
2. "I slammed the crooked door shut and watched as the cereal boxes on top of the fridge wobbled, and then toppled off."
3. "Suddenly, four men dressed in all black sped around then darted around the corner."

Of course, the students all saw this as tedious work at first, but they soon realized that some of their peers either had fabulous details showing certain aspects of their stories or weak and/or missing evidence of the same. They used this new information to edit their own stories and to self-assess. After using this format for several

Figure 3a ▼

Editor's Name _____   Writer's Name _____

Proofreading Exercise for Creative Writing

As peer editors, each of you will peruse (read carefully) at least two students' works and identify aspects of each according to the chart below. It is vital to provide constructive criticism, or warm and cool feedback. Don't simply say, "Nice job!" and draw a little smiley face. Become both teacher and critic, and through this you will improve your writing. You must use the constructive criticism of your peers to improve your piece; if you're unsure about it, see me.

WARM SIDE!!!

Place: Identify **two** showing details that take you to this place.
1. _____
2. _____

Character: Identify **two** showing details that help you experience who these characters are.
1. _____
2. _____

Dialogue: Identify **two** strong examples of real use of dialogue.
1. _____
2. _____

Action: Identify **two** showing details that help you to see or perceive the action.
1. _____
2. _____

Conflict: Identify the **major** conflict of this story.
_____
_____

Resolution: How is this conflict resolved?
_____
_____

Write two examples of strong, showing word choice.
1. _____
2. _____

Identify **two** well-crafted phrases or sentences that enhance the story.
1. _____
2. _____

COOL SIDE

Write **two** examples of weak, telling (not showing) word choice.
1. _____
2. _____

Place: Identify **two** telling (not showing) details that try to describe this place.
1. _____
2. _____

Character: Identify **two** telling (not showing) details about these characters.
1. _____
2. _____

Dialogue: Identify **two** weak examples of dialogue.
1. _____
2. _____

Action: Identify **two** telling (not showing) details about action.
1. _____
2. _____

Identify **two** weak phrases that are confusing and/or don't follow the story.
1. _____
2. _____

Check the column that applies to the category.

	Excellent	Good	Average	Poor
Showing details				
Organization (effective beginning and ending)				
Cohesion				
Voice				
Sense of character, action, and place				
Word choice				
Grammar				

Comment on any of those categories.
_____
_____

Also suggest ways of improving this piece...
_____
_____

See pages 112 and 113 for Blackline Master

"Students quickly learned the value of quality over quantity..."

stories and alternating groups, students had assessed a wide range of writers and found strong, helpful examples as well as reminders of what not to do. Self-assessment is the key to student improvement. After using rubrics to assess classmates' work, all of my students became proficient in interpreting and properly using the writing rubric.

This was especially important, given the abstract nature of short stories and the difficulties found in assessing them. Students quickly learned the value of quality over quantity when a few tightly written two-page stories received a higher score than some ten-plus-page stories that fell short according to criteria generated by the class.

Immediate student feedback, though, provided me with the need for more critical rubrics, especially for peer assessment. My students told me that too much of the rubric was positive; they wanted to know where their writing was weak so they could properly fix it. This outcry forced me to re-examine the rubric we had created together. I reduced the number of examples from three to two when looking for evidence of criteria and added a cool side to the back of the sheet with the same set of criteria for constructive criticism (Figure 3a). Not until they began to use these new expanded rubrics did the students realize their huge mistake – they had actually created more work for themselves! Nevertheless, the new rubric helped them to produce better quality stories. Their feedback to each other became more specific and more helpful (Figure 3b).

Editor's Name _____   Writer's Name _____

Proofreading Exercise for Creative Writing

As peer editors, each of you will peruse (read carefully) at least two students' works and identify aspects of each according to the chart below. It is vital to provide constructive criticism, or warm and cool feedback. Don't simply say, "Nice job!" and draw a little smiley face. Become both teacher and critic, and through this you will improve your writing. You must use the constructive criticism of your peers to improve your piece; if you're unsure about it, see me.

WARM SIDE!!!

Character: Identify **two** showing details that help you experience who these characters are.

1. He was thirty nine year old man with a new convertable.

2. Very skinny with very long arms and legs.

Dialogue: Identify **two** strong examples of real use of dialogue.

1. "Can I interest you in something to drink."

2. "I'll take some soda if you have," scot replied.

Action: Identify **two** showing details that help you to see or perceive the action.

1. as he reached back his arm knocked off a jar of peach jam.

2. The jam smashed and the jam splattered onto the floor.

COOL SIDE

Character: Identify **two** telling (not showing) details about these characters.

1. wore brown shorts that covered his thick thighs.

2. His shirt was damp with sweat build up.

Dialogue: Identify **two** weak examples of dialogue.

1. "Hey, listen to this," Randy blurted out.

2. "Shoot," Clarence yelled.

Action: Identify **two** telling (not showing) details about action.

1. went hunting in the woods.

2. I shot a big deer.

Poetry Writing

Just when I thought I had the assessment of story writing down, I dared to introduce a poetry writing unit. This was met with much chagrin; students gagged, chortled, cried, sighed, complained, and threatened to drop the class. I quickly reminded them that this was, in fact, Creative Writing 1, and that they had signed on for more than just story writing. A few were elated at the thought of finally writing poetry, but they were in the minority by a long shot. So, there I was, unsure of how to proceed, let alone how to assess, this no-rules form of writing.

Being a rookie writing teacher, I knew I couldn't tackle this enormous obstacle alone. I called for reinforcements, and luckily, I found Susan Conley, a local published poet, who agreed to talk to the students about writing poetry. I didn't know if she were a centenarian with half-moon glasses or a new-age beat poet; I wondered if she were, in fact, the answer that I needed. When she arrived, Susan made the most profound yet simple statement I have heard about writing poetry: *"Writing a poem is the same thing as writing a story using a different form."* Boom – there it was! Storywriters could easily be poets. They just had to put their stories into lines of verse. Suddenly the doors flew open. After several sensory activities, such as jot-listing every notion associated with the phrase "live chickens," a class of mostly reluctant poets was discovering the muse within each of them.

Susan Conley unlocked an essential secret – poetry can be fun! By sharing her own published work and breaking some of it down to show the importance of line breaks and word choice, she helped my students become believers in themselves – they too could write poetry. For many of them, it was like pouring melted cheddar cheese on unwanted broccoli – it suddenly tasted great.

Figure 4 ▼

Writer's Name _____

Poetry Rubric

After writing your awesome poetry, assess it and show evidence using this form.

Identify three excellent sounds and images from your poems.
1. *"Heart engulfed by flame"*
2. *"Rests its head on a black cloud"*
3. *"And day's warmth is replaced by night's deathly cold"*

Identify four different examples of literary devices.
1. *Simile "Like a stone"*
2. *Repetition "Her smile, her laugh, her voice, her hair"*
3. *Metaphor "Fades with the setting sun"*
4. *Symbol "sunset"*

Write three examples of strong, showing word choice.
1. *"Ragged"*
2. *"Shrouded"*
3. *"Engulfed"*

Identify three well-crafted lines (strong, showing lines)
1. *"And as the sun is consumed by darkness"*
2. *"Through summer's moon bleeds a crimson red"*
3. *"Bleeding onto the leaves that now lie dead"*

Editor _____
Writer's Name _____

Poetry Rubric

After writing your awesome poetry, assess it and show evidence using this form.

Identify three excellent sounds and images from your poems.
1. *"as light flows out dark rushes in."*
2. *"the fire / in the back of my imagination."*
3. *"screams too small to hear"*

Identify four different examples of literary devices.
1. *"Dying leaves take their last breaths"*
2. *"I waited / like a stone"*
3. *"My statue crumbled to fall"*
4. *"Summer's moon bleeds through crimson"*

Write three examples of strong, showing word choice.
1. *"engulfed"*
2. *"shrouded"*
3. *"ragged"*

Identify three well-crafted lines (strong, showing lines)
1. *"the lost souls / they watch me burn"*
2. *"Rests its head on a black cloud"*
3. *"a chilling silence replaces summer's din"*

So, my students had become poets overnight, but I had the new issue of how to assess their poetry. This is especially difficult in a diverse class of college/honors and freshman/sophomore students. To complicate matters further, a few students were natural and prolific poets, whereas the rest were novices at best. How could I possibly assess their poetry using the same rubric?

Clearly I needed help, so I asked my colleagues for their rubrics, but none seemed to fit. I felt I couldn't even modify them to meet my needs and the needs of my students. Then I asked my students, and after having read a variety of poetry, we created criteria for the poems by listing qualities that described what we felt good poetry looked and sounded like. They provided critical input, such as the need for literary devices, word choice, sounds and images, central theme or idea, and so on.

With my guidance, we transformed this list into a rubric and created a peer-edit sheet, which they also used to self-assess and provide evidence in each category, showing how they met or exceeded the criteria. Doing this demonstrated that they understood what each criterion meant and required; if there were a misunderstanding, it would be apparent in the self-assessment and could be rectified through conversation with myself or peers. After two major poetry assignments (totaling a minimum of 150 lines), clear criteria, and peer and self-assessment, all my students were amazed with the poetry they had produced.

Showing Evidence

I believe the key to demonstrating the understanding of concepts is showing evidence. Once my students (with my guidance) had decided what good participation or poetry looks like, had modeled both strong and weak examples and had practiced using the rubrics, they were able to self-assess and show evidence for each criterion on their list. When the evidence shown didn't match the criteria in the rubric, the details easily identified the breakdown in understanding of that particular concept. Evidence is the link between expectations and student understanding.

The bottom line with self-assessment and criteria setting is student buy-in. By allowing our students, with teacher guidance, to create the requirements for the assessment, we as their teachers are empowering them to make seemingly huge decisions. Often they create criteria that may be more involved than we had initially expected; if the converse is true, then we can simply make adjustments as necessary. When the students set criteria, they immediately understand the expectations of the assessment and will have more enthusiasm for the assignment. Their input is valued, and they have a voice in determining the most important aspects of their assessment. Also, student choice in writing creatively helps foster more passion and ardor in the work.

"The key to demonstrating the understanding of concepts is showing evidence."

Assessing the unassessable seems impossible at first, but we, as educators, must ask ourselves and our students this essential question: What are the most important criteria to be expected in abstract assignments, and how can they be met and/or exceeded? By defining criteria with our students first, we encourage student buy-in and help them to self-assess and improve the quality of their work. Through self-assessment, our students will demonstrate their skills and understanding of the concepts and knowledge learned, and we will receive valuable feedback about the assessment itself.

Philip Divinsky has been a classroom teacher at Portland Arts and Technology High School in Maine for over 15 years. His expertise is working with students with special needs in a vocational setting, and he has facilitated workshops on classroom management and assessment. In his other life, Phil has been a professional musician for 30 years. He is the Portland program coordinator and teacher for Guitars in the Classroom, a national organization that focuses on helping teachers use music in their classrooms.

Philip Divinsky & Tom Lafavore

Tom Lafavore, M.Ed., C.A.S., was a high school and middle school teacher for over 25 years. He has consulted with Maine school districts on assessment, curriculum, and instruction, and provided professional development in those areas to individual schools and districts. He has also been an elementary and secondary principal. As the current Director of Educational Planning for Portland (Maine) Public Schools, Tom provides assessment, curriculum, and instructional support to Portland's educators. He is also completing work toward his doctorate in Educational Leadership at the University of Maine.

Creating the Classroom Culture
by Philip Divinsky

It's the first day of classes in a new school year. As you prepare to meet students for the first time, you wonder how nervous they will be and how you can help their transition into a new school and new class. You greet each student at the door with a smile and welcoming hello. As the class settles down and students find a seat in the horseshoe-shaped seating arrangement, you introduce yourself and ask them to introduce themselves to the rest of the class. And so it begins.

This describes the beginning of my first day of school for the past 13 or so years. I teach at Portland Arts and Technology High School, a regional vocational school in Portland, Maine. We serve 23 high schools, with some students traveling as long as an hour to take classes at our school. Our food service class is called Fast Foods and geared for students with special needs. These students have an incredibly wide variety of abilities. Some students are non-readers and some are at grade-level academics; others are non-talkers and behaviorally challenged individuals. In this chapter, I would like to share with you some strategies I use to create a classroom where all individuals are respected, where students have a say in what and how they learn, and where giving and getting quality, timely feedback is the focus of assessment for learning.

Before we begin, let's talk about time. In our class, we spend days, sometimes weeks, creating our classroom culture. I have had teachers and administrators ask questions like, "How can you spend so much time not teaching your subject matter?" These questions are even more prevalent under the weight of *No Child Left Behind.* My contention is that by spending the time *up front* to teach cooperative skills and create a respectful learning environment, teachers will save time over the course of the year.

Most teachers have a bag of tricks – strategies that work for them to get students comfortable in their class. Here are a few that I use that seem to work for my students.

CONTENTS

Charting

The first few days of school, I ask the students the following questions and chart their responses.

Figure 1 ▼

What are the qualities of your favorite classes?
What are the qualities of your favorite teachers?
What do you want to learn in our class?

These charts are then posted in the classroom. The chart that lists the qualities of their favorite teachers is posted on my door. This lets the students know that I respect and honor their views. I refer to these charts throughout the school year, reminding the students that these charts are their work. This is the students' first experience of brainstorming criteria, as well as contributing to their learning destinations for the year.

Figure 2 ▼

Introductions by Interview

I ask students who don't know each other to pair up and interview the other person. We preface this with developing interview questions together. Again, we are having the students set criteria for the work they will be doing. Each student then introduces the student whom they interviewed to the class.

The Name Game

While standing in a circle, students toss a Nerf or tennis ball to another student or teacher. The student must say the person's name to whom they are throwing. It is important to set some safety rules such as being aware of your surroundings, only throwing underhand and tossing gently. If the thrower does not know the name of a person, they are encouraged to ask that person his or her name. The physical act of throwing, while saying the person's name and looking at them, contributes to remembering names quickly.

All-Inclusive Classroom Contracts

Modeled after *Expeditionary Learning Full-Value Contracts* (see www.elob.org), this is a process where the students and the teacher create a contract that states the kinds of behaviors that need to be happening in our classroom, in order to have a successful learning environment. This is another way to involve students in shaping their learning destination and creating criteria. It is also important to state what kinds of behaviors would be barriers to learning and cooperation. When the contract is created, it can either be written out

Figure 3 ▼

on poster paper or creatively stated, using pictures, drawings and words. We discuss what it means to sign a contract, and that by signing the document, we are agreeing to abide by the contract for the school year. We then have our signing ceremony. The contract is displayed in a very visible area of the classroom so we can refer to it whenever necessary.

Ice Breaking Games (task-oriented)

Simple challenges (such as, lining up by age, by shoe size, or by height, with time limits) provide a fun way for students to learn to work together and gives the teacher a glimpse at who might have emerging leadership tendencies in the class. Other games, such as timing how long it takes to pass a ball around the whole circle and continuously trying to beat the record, or finding quicker ways to move the ball, can be added to the mix. Processing, or debriefing the group dynamic immediately afterwards, is critical to the learning process. Here is where we set the stage for giving and receiving feedback. Students are asked what went well and how they might improve. We practice talking to each other respectfully, giving praise or constructive critiques. When teachers model what this looks like, students typically catch on very quickly.

"By spending the time up front to teach cooperative skills and create a respectful learning environment, teachers will save time over the course of the year."

Final Thoughts

These are just some ways teachers can create a safe atmosphere for learning and taking risks. As well, teachers establish a culture for a classroom where giving and receiving timely, specific feedback is valued as a productive way to learn and do our best work.

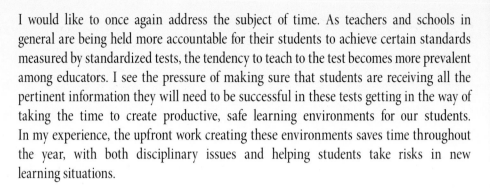

I would like to once again address the subject of time. As teachers and schools in general are being held more accountable for their students to achieve certain standards measured by standardized tests, the tendency to teach to the test becomes more prevalent among educators. I see the pressure of making sure that students are receiving all the pertinent information they will need to be successful in these tests getting in the way of taking the time to create productive, safe learning environments for our students. In my experience, the upfront work creating these environments saves time throughout the year, with both disciplinary issues and helping students take risks in new learning situations.

"I want them to have a belief in themselves that they are capable of great things."

A guiding question for me in this work is: *What qualities and skills do I, as an educator, want our students to have?* Surely I want them to be knowledgeable. I want them to produce quality products. I want them to be able to communicate effectively in a variety of different ways. I want them to be involved with their community. I want to help them gain a love for learning that lasts throughout their lifetimes. I want them to learn to work collaboratively with both their peers and adults. I want them to have a belief in themselves that they are capable of great things.

I believe that by creating a learning environment where it is safe to take risks, where feedback is valued and used as an effective assessment tool and where students are encouraged to take part in deciding how and what they learn, we are facilitating the process for our students to acquire the qualities we would like them to possess for their future.

Parts to Whole - Whole to Parts: An Administrator's Perspective
by Thomas Lafavore

It has been four years since I have been in front of a classroom full of students, but I love visiting classrooms to re-experience learners in action. I find myself in the Fast Foods class quite often. These students have formed themselves into a working team that consistently demonstrates their knowledge and skills. They recognize their own strengths, and work in an environment where they feel confident to take risks. It is an environment that recognizes that each student is an individual and, at the same time, individuals work together to complete the task at hand. Such recognition explores the uniqueness of the parts, helps them become whole as a team, but never loses sight of their individuality.

As I explore teaching and learning in other classrooms, I fear that teachers who understand the wisdom and effectiveness of differentiation forget the importance of teamwork. While a differentiated classroom helps individual learners gain knowledge and skills at a level and through a method that best suits that learner, educators should not abandon the sense of team, in a quest to explore differences. It is when the differences that represent each student's unique strengths are built upon and used to support one another collaboratively, that educators are preparing students to face the world beyond the school.

Another reason I visit the Fast Foods classroom is to assure myself that recent policy and mandates have little or no connection to teaching and learning. As I observe students in this class offer critical feedback to one another, as I observe them perform their daily tasks, and as I welcome their smiles, I wonder what we have done. In a world that cannot see beyond the bottom line of test scores, I become aware that recent policies have abandoned the parts and only want the whole. If you really want to assess learning, visit Phil's class for a day. In that class, everyone makes sure that *no one is left behind!*

"It is when the differences that represent each student's unique strengths are built upon and used to support one another collaboratively, that educators are preparing students to face the world beyond the school."

Stephanie Doane

Stephanie Doane, B.A., M.S.Ed., is an experienced high school educator with a strong background in assessment practice and social studies curriculum development. She is the recipient of the Maine 2003 James Madison Memorial Fellowship for Constitutional Studies, and has consulted at the state level in the development of state standards in social studies. Stephanie currently teaches 10th grade humanities at Casco Bay High School, Maine's first Expeditionary Learning/Outward Bound high school.

Promoting Lifelong Learning: Creative Assessment Practices in Social Studies
by Stephanie Doane

The time has come to shift our focus from testing to students, and high school teachers can do this in the place where they know their students best – the classroom. By creating classroom assessment systems that promote learning rather than stifle, that allow creativity to flourish rather than wither, teachers can create for their secondary students a learning experience that better reflects the world of today. By involving secondary students in the classroom assessment process, we can counter the negative effects of high-stakes tests and construct learning environments that invite students to actively participate in their own learning, engage in deep thinking and promote creative problem solving.

How can involving students in the assessment process counter the negative effects of high-stakes testing while supporting the development of future success for all learners? By using assessment in a formative manner, that is *throughout* the learning process rather than just at the *end* of learning, teachers can quickly become informed in regard to student strengths and needs. By actively involving secondary students in this process, students develop an awareness of self that will not only support success in the classroom, but also in the world outside of school. Together, using formative assessment practices, students and teachers can make the assessment process a dynamic one that supports personal growth, risk-taking and self-discovery. This also helps to develop in students the ability to continue learning into, and hopefully throughout, adulthood. In the complex world we live in today, the ability to continue learning beyond the years of formal schooling is imperative for success.

My own journey to create such dynamic learning experiences for my students continues to this day. Early on in my teaching career I realized that assessment, when used in a formative manner, could instruct and facilitate understanding. I developed assessment practices that frequently checked for understanding and gave students the opportunity to act on teacher-provided feedback. I encouraged students to revise work products based on the feedback provided, and I would re-evaluate the work until we were satisfied. After attending several assessment conferences and taking a class specifically on student-involved classroom assessment, I developed and put into practice an assessment system that fully involves and invites students to self-assess, be reflective and take risks as learners. I realized through my own reflection that what I was creating for my students was a learning environment that was accepting of mistakes. So often our assessment system punishes such risk-taking and in the process, may limit and narrow learning. I realized that if I really wanted my students to grow as learners, I had to create a safe environment, one in which students would be willing to risk attempting more and more challenging tasks. I have been purposefully working to involve students in classroom assessment now for seven years and I know of no better way to support creative and critical learning for *all students*.

Listed below are just a few of the specific ways teachers can involve high school students in the classroom assessment process:

Student Use of Progress Portfolios

At the beginning of each course give students time to create portfolios, in which they organize evidence of their learning, in the form of four-pocket portfolios. These progress portfolios differ from many portfolios used in elementary and middle school – they focus exclusively on the course learning goals. Have students label three pockets with clear learning goals established by the teacher, and label one pocket with a student-set learning goal for the course. The portfolios stay in the classroom and students visit them periodically in order to organize evidence of learning, as well as self-assess progress toward the learning goals. Students select evidence from their ongoing class work that demonstrates progress, growth or achievement within the learning goal. For example, a learning goal might be to become a more proficient writer and evidence of progress toward that goal could be a series of improved scores on test essays.

I encourage students to keep examples of past work, even if the work is not their best, because the focus of the progress portfolio is *progress*. The portfolios can also serve as a basis for conversations with the student about their learning. At the end of the course, students use the portfolios filled with evidence of learning to support success on a reflective final exam (explained later) or summary of the course (see below).

Figure 1 ▼

Student-Involved Conferences

Figure 2 ▼

A few weeks into each course, I ask students to participate in a conference on their progress using the format set forth in *Conferencing and Reporting* by Gregory, Cameron and Davies (2001). Students have prepared for the conference by previously visiting their portfolio and placing in it their early evidence of learning. The conversation should focus on student learning and evidence of that learning (from the portfolio). This gives both the teacher and the student the opportunity to either affirm or adjust the learning goals (from the progress portfolio) based on feedback from those involved in the conference.

Use of Student-Set Criteria

In most secondary classrooms, teachers establish the criteria that are used to evaluate student work products. Another approach that involves students more directly in 'owning' the criteria is to invite students, with guidance from the teacher, to establish the criteria for major work products (reports, presentations, investigations, demonstrations, exhibitions, and essays). The criteria can then be used to create rubrics, checklists, and other tools for peer and self-assessment, while the work is in progress. The same criteria can be used in final teacher evaluations by assigning value (both numeric and descriptive) to the student work based on the criteria. A process for involving students in criteria setting is laid out in *Setting and Using Criteria* by Gregory, Cameron and Davies (1997). This technique is especially useful for supporting student success on long-term projects and group work. For example, early in the school year, I help students set criteria for group work using the prompt *"What makes a good group worker?"* All group work is then evaluated using these criteria.

Figure 3 ▼

	Student-set group work criteria*	
2nd block US History and the Modern World		**3rd block US History and the Modern World**
1. Participated and had good attendance.		1. Is dependable, comes prepared and shares responsibility equally.
2. Did fair share of work and fulfilled responsibilities,		2. Is a collaborative worker, cooperates, participates and is flexible.
3. Picked up the slack when necessary.		3. Makes an effort to contribute, to be creative and innovative.
4. Brought in constructive ideas		4. Has respect for others, is a good listener and accepts others ideas.
5. Is open-minded and cooperative with others		5. Has a positive attitude.

Students use the criteria to self-assess and give focused feedback to their peers.

Use of Student "check-ins" on Long-Term Projects

Long term projects are always stressful, especially when tossed into the busy lives of today's high school students. Whenever students are involved in a project that requires days or weeks to complete, periodically "check-in" with students. Take the time to ask each student (during class) how things are going, what still needs to be done and what problems they foresee to successful completion of the project. While check-ins do not require that the student necessarily produce evidence, it is a great way for students to assess their own progress. By sharing this information as a class, students have the opportunity to self-assess and learn from their peers. As their teacher, you can get a sense of student progress on the project as well.

Opportunities for Students to Act on Descriptive Feedback

If feedback is going to support student learning, then students need the opportunity to act on that feedback. Build into your course assessment system the understanding that students should and will act on all forms of feedback, including teacher feedback. This can apply to class work, projects, writing assignments and tests. In many high school classrooms, teachers evaluate work products, hand the product with the evaluative feedback back to the student and that is it.

But that is not where the learning should end. In fact, feedback becomes much more valuable when students know that they have the opportunity to use it as a guide to improve their work product. If corrections or changes are needed, students use the descriptive feedback to make the necessary changes, then submit the product for evaluation. If you wish to promote a learning environment which encourages risk-taking then you should not apply a penalty for initial mistakes. Rather, focus on the progress and learning that has occurred as a result of student effort.

"A reflective final grants students the opportunity to identify patterns of growth…"

Opportunities for Students to be Reflective

At points throughout the course, give students the opportunity to stop and be reflective about learning that has taken place thus far, as well as the learning to come. Consider, as well, the use of a *reflective final* rather than a comprehensive final in the exam format (see Figure 4). A reflective final gives students the opportunity to self-assess in a comprehensive manner at a crucial time – before they leave your class. A reflective final grants students the opportunity to identify patterns of growth and communicate their learning in an authentic format. It gives you the opportunity to see each student's learning in a format focused on evidence and arranged in such a way that supports the learning goals of the class. Teachers can then use the opportunity to determine a final course grade that is truly reflective of student progress and growth – something that may not always occur if the final course grade is dependent solely on student work products or tests.

Figure 4 ▼

Final Exam: Reflective Summary   Name _____
Doane – US in the Modern World

Directions: 1. Use your **progress portfolios** as your source of evidence.
                     2. Follow the directions under each heading.
                     3. Place evidence, reflections and evidence for reflections in portfolio and submit as your final exam.

I. DESTINATIONS	II. CONTENT UNITS
• proficient writer • productive researcher • collaborative group worker • (student created)	• African-American Experience in the 20th Century • Boom and Bust in 20th Century America • 20th Century American Legal History • America Becomes a World Power • Modern Foreign Policy: Vietnam and Iraq

A. Evidence

1. Find and organize evidence that demonstrates growth, progress or achievement in **each of the 4 destinations.**

2. Label each accordingly using the post-it notes.

3. Place the evidence in the appropriate pocket.

B. Reflection

1. **Choose one destination** in which you feel you grew or achieved the most.

2. Reflectively write about your growth or achievement in that area addressing the following prompts:

• *Specifically how have you grown or achieved in this area? (Discuss evidence)*
• *Why is this skill or area important?*
• *How could you use this skill or area in the future?*

3. Find and label **evidence** that supports your assertions.

4. Place the reflection and evidence within the first portfolio.

A. Evidence

1. Find and organize evidence that demonstrates growth, progress or achievement in **4 content units.**

2. Label each accordingly using the post-it notes.

3. Place the evidence in the appropriate pocket.

B. Reflection

1. **Choose one content unit** in which you feel you grew or achieved the most.

2. Reflectively write about your growth or achievement in that area addressing the following prompts:

• *Specifically what have you learned about America from studying this unit? (Discuss evidence)*
• *Why is this information important?*
• *How could you use this information or way of understanding America in the future?*

3. Find and label **evidence** that supports your assertions.

4. Place the reflection and evidence within the second portfolio.

Trying to capture the power of these practices in writing is difficult. Even more difficult is the implementation of these practices, especially in high schools, where so often the focus is on the learning of content to support success on summative assessments rather than creative instruction to support complex thinking. Yet, it is imperative that we take positive action to better prepare young adults for the world that awaits them outside of high school.

This is a world that expects results and demands evidence to support the results. By involving secondary students in the classroom assessment process, we are promoting not just creative thinking and learning, but accountability as well. We are supporting accountability in its most **dependable** form – evidence that demonstrates the learning behind any summative numbers or grades.

Works Cited

Gregory K., Cameron C. & Davies A. (2001). *Knowing What Counts: Conferencing and Reporting.* Courtenay, BC.: Connections Publishing.

Gregory K., Cameron C. & Davies A. (1997). *Knowing What Counts: Setting and Using Criteria.* Courtenay, BC.: Connections Publishing.

Alice Yates

Alice Yates, B.S., M.S.Ed., is an experienced educator in French and Art at secondary and post-secondary levels. After extensive studies in assessment practices and Teaching Proficiency through Reading and Storytelling (formerly called Total Physical Response with Storytelling – an innovative methodology for language acquisition), she has blended the two techniques into an effective strategy for teaching high school students. Alice has presented district-wide workshops in brain-based research assessment practices and has organized conferences with Blaine Ray, inventor of TPRS, for the New England area language teachers. She is the administrator for her school district's Foreign Language Assistance Program grant.

Making Assessment & Instruction Work in a Modern Language Classroom

by Alice Yates

I danced, sang, clapped, mimed, and chanted my way through verb charts and vocabulary lists for seventeen years. Multiple intelligences aside, it wasn't working – not for me, not for my students. I knew my students were capable of speaking, reading, listening, and writing better. The textbook approach, plus endless supplements, was not getting the students where they wanted to be – able to use the language with some ease. Luckily, Blaine Ray, inventor of *Teaching Proficiency through Reading and Storytelling* (TPRS), was invited to our state conference about five years ago. He offered a common sense, research-based approach to language acquisition, not language learning. At the same time, our district was asked to send volunteers to Anne Davies' *Learning Connections Assessment Symposium* on Vancouver Island, BC, Canada. That spring and summer impacted my classroom in a revolutionary way.

It had always seemed easier to start over by listening to the latest research instead of trying to adapt the new into the old. I threw out the textbook, retrained with Blaine Ray and his colleagues, and rewrote assessments using Anne Davies, Kathleen Gregory, and Caren Cameron as my sources of inspiration. I had to ask myself how to incorporate the assessments *for* learning with language *acquisition* through storytelling.

First and foremost, TPRS calls for comprehensible input. Students acquire language by listening to *understandable*, repetitive phrases. For years, language teachers have been using charades to avoid speaking English in the classroom. Sometimes those charades go on for seven minutes or longer. Why spend that much time pantomiming a word or expression when it would take two seconds to stop the lesson or story and say what it means in English? The repetitive structures of TPRS are deliberately bizarre and/or personalized to the class through the context of a story to aid long-term memory retention. The **three steps of TPRS** are:

1. **Establish Meaning** by writing three to four phrases, in both the native language and the target language, where all can see them.

2. **"Ask"** a story by eliciting student responses to repetitive questions that focus on the key phrases. Interest in the story is kept through personalizing the story to the class and including fun/strange details. Cognates are used heavily to enhance the story without adding new vocabulary. At all times, question words and phrases are posted on the walls of the classroom in both native and target language, to facilitate "asking" the story.

3. **Reading** a follow-up page that contains the same vocabulary as the "story" provides further input that cements sentence structure and vocabulary in the brain. It also helps introduce new words through contextual clues. Readers with repetitive phrases and single-page stories work well for beginning as well as advanced students.

Briefly, a sample lesson would be three phrases such as: *the dog went, the bank was closed, the cat was sad.* The teacher might ask: *Who went to the bank* (a cognate, depending on the target language)? *The dog went where? Did the dog go to the store? No, the dog didn't go to the store; the dog went to the bank. Did an elephant go to the bank? No, the elephant didn't go to the bank; the dog went to the bank. Did the dog or the giraffe go to the bank? Oh yes, the dog went to the bank.* By now, there are 10 repetitions of the phrase *went to the bank* in either a positive or negative format. The teacher may feel as if the phrase has been beaten into the ground at this point, but many of the students are still trying to acquire *went to the bank*.

Adding details keeps interest for the auditory students who pick up the language more quickly and for the teacher. *The dog who went to the bank, was he big or small? Yes, he was* very small, super small, super, super small. Why did the super, super small dog go to the bank? He wanted money so he went to the bank? Why did he want money? He went to the bank because he wanted money to buy a super small car for his girlfriend?

(Hopefully, the students are giving these details, and if not, the teacher has a skeletal story outline in mind.) *There was a problem, class, oh no! The bank was closed! Where was the bank? The bank was closed in Tight Wad, Missouri? Why was the bank closed? It was Martin Luther King, Jr. Day and the bank was closed? No? It was July 4th and the bank was closed? Why was the bank closed? The bank was closed because it was Sunday. The bank was closed because it was Sunday or Monday? Yes, it was closed because it was Sunday.* (That's the idea – *the cat was sad* would be repeated the same way and trying to weave it into the "story.")

A reading page that has a story using the same key phrases then follows the "asked" story. Students read a paragraph at a time and are asked questions about the reading and questions that make connections with their own lives, i.e. *Who has a dog? Did your dog go to the bank? What did you do on Sunday?* and so on.

"…the teacher is searching for the glazed-over looks of incomprehension in the eyes of students…"

Assessment with TPRS

Class observations are continuous. While "asking" the story and teaching to the eyes, the teacher is searching for the glazed-over looks of incomprehension in the eyes of students – assessing in the midst of learning. A quick translation usually readjusts that look. Another assessment observation technique is to ask for a show of fingers, i.e. show 10 fingers if 100% is understood, 9 fingers for 90%, and so on. If students are showing 7 or fewer fingers, it is necessary to stop and revisit the previous sentences or phrases in the class story. Quizzes often ask students to draw the meanings of phrases; for example, when students draw a picture of "she heard," it is usually a stick figure of a girl with a big ear and an arrow going towards the ear. This pushes for more right-brain activity and creativity, as well as fewer translations from one language to another. An example of a writing assessment is a timed writing. At the beginning of the year, students are given ten minutes to write an essay or story in the target language. Minutes are shaved off the time as students become more comfortable with the process. By the end of the year, most level two to four students are able to

Figure 1 ▼

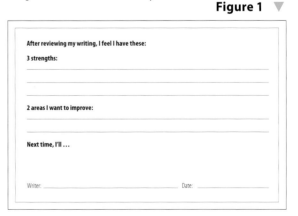

After reviewing my writing, I feel I have these:

3 strengths:
_____
_____
_____

2 areas I want to improve:
_____
_____

Next time, I'll …
_____

Writer: _____ Date: _____

See page 114 for Blackline Master

Figure 2 ▼

After listening to you, I understood:

3 things:

_____

_____

_____

2 questions I have:

_____

_____

Next time, I'd like to add . . .

_____

Writer: _____   Date: _____

See page 115 for Blackline Master

Figure 3 ▼

Après avoir vu _____ en français:
                (After having seen . . .)

J'ai compris (I understood) ces 3 choses (things) essentielles:

1.
2.
3.

J'ai entendu (heard) ces mots ou ces expressions:

_____   _____   _____
_____   _____   _____
_____   _____   _____
_____   _____   _____
_____   _____   _____

J'ai des questions ou Je n'ai pas compris:

_____

Ma partie favorite était: (My favorite part was . . .)

_____

Nom: _____   Date: _____

See page 116 for Blackline Master

Figure 4 ▼

Home Performance by _____ Date: le _____
                    (Devoirs pour la classe de français)

I will tell the story, _____
Please notice:

And watch for :

Body Language   Acting   Speaking French   Eye Contact   Enthusiasm

Home Audience Response by _____

After listening to and watching your storytelling, I'd like to specifically compliment you on:

_____

_____

See page 117 for Blackline Master

write 100+ words in paragraph format, in the target language, during five minutes – a sign of a fluent writer (according to Susan Gross).

Students are excited by their progress in quantity, but they need to go a step further by reflecting on their writing in order to improve the quality. The author reads aloud his or her timed writing to a student partner, which allows for auditory processing. When the self-reflection is added, students focus on their writing strengths, areas to improve, and set a goal for their next writing piece (Figure 1).

The bonus to this process is the opportunity for the listener to write three things that were understood, some questions for the author, and specific feedback. The listener shares this information with the writer and keeps the reflection as listening evidence. I see my students taking their writing more seriously since they are required to reflect on it, and because they know a peer will be listening to their work (Figure 2).

My students and I have created self-reflection assessments in the other content standard areas of reading, speaking, listening/viewing, and cultural connections. The reading entry log expects students to record the pages read in their readers, along with the main idea, supporting details, and vocabulary learned (Figure 3). Other reading logs are used to jot brief notes about books selected and read during free reading time. Students suggested doing current events in a way that could be better documented and used as proof of reading and/or making cultural connections. One of the students created the format; it was approved by the others, and is currently serving its purpose well.

The speaking evidence is a performance-style feedback response form to which the students recently added a self-reflective rubric (Figure 4). They decided on the criteria for a speaker in either a storytelling situation or a conversation. They expanded the criteria to indicate progress in "content," "speaking target language," "flow," and "pronunciation." The ability to be understood was the critical factor in each of the selected parameters (Figure 5).

Figure 5 ▼

| Name: _____ | | |
| Class: _____ | | |

Self-Assessment Speaking	4 Exceeds	3 Meets
Content: Conversation Storytelling	Content completely understandable, no errors ⟶ deep content/answer ⟶ rich details ⟶ asks interesting questions	Content mostly understandable, few errors ⟶ adequate content/answer ⟶ some details ⟶ asks questions
I Speak Target Language with:	Broad vocabulary, no English — use complex sentences with multi-tenses	Strong vocabulary, little English, can improvise — use simple and complex sentences with tense changes
Flow:	Speaking flows without hesitation	Speaking flows fairly smoothly
Pronunciation:	Accent is understandable, distinct voice	Accent is understandable, no mumbling

Upon reflection of my speaking French today, I:

_____

_____

Next time while speaking, I want to focus on:

_____

_____

The listening/viewing reflective piece has also seen an update to include more space for the vocabulary understood, plus a section for making cultural connections, between the featured culture and the student's own culture/life (Figure 6). They also use a running log for cultural notes that cites the source, who or what culture, time period, what is like us and what is different from us.

Classroom observations self reflections, journals, quizzes, and portfolios are complemented by quarterly conferencing with the teacher. This permits triangulation of evidence observations, products, and conversations about student progress. Student led conferences are also held school-wide in the fall for goal-setting purposes with their invited guests. School wide showcase exhibitions in

Figure 6 ▼

Après avoir vu _____ en français:
(After having seen . . .)

Continué . . .
J'ai entendu (heard) ces mots ou ces expressions:

_____   _____   _____
_____   _____   _____
_____   _____   _____
_____   _____   _____
_____   _____   _____
_____   _____   _____

J'ai remarqué (noticed) ces choses d'un autre culture et je fais une comparaison entre (between)
l'autre culture et mon culture : (en français ou en anglais) (. . . legal issues, employment, work habits,
rituals, politics, sports, leisure activities, cultural values, socially acceptable behaviors, etc.)

Figure 7 ▼

Possible Evidence of Writing in Target Language	
Weblog	Poetry
Write answers to survey/questions	Short stories
Write notes or short letters	Long stories
Journals	Essays
Letters	Summaries
E-mail or hardcopy to penpal	Technical writing
Simple story — everyday life	Persuasive writing
Write a personal opinion w. explanation	1-2 pages research report
Analytical writing / compare & contrast	

Type of evidence:
I am able to . . . .(link ability to evidence)

_____

_____

_____

Name: _____ **Date:** _____

the spring are celebrations of goals being met and demonstrations of knowledge with evidence, reflections, and new goals for further progress.

Recent conversations with Anne Davies about the individual quarterly conferences led me to create continua with my students for each of the standards. We spent a good deal of time working on them using their ideas and the Maine State Learning Results for Modern and Classical Languages The students suggested ways to better *prove* their learning as they thought about the progression a reader, writer, listener, or speaker makes as the skills grow. We also wanted to have documents that are user-friendlier than the Maine Learning Results, which is a comprehensive plan, but awkward for students to use. Every student downloaded the resulting continua and added icons to show their current ability level, allowing them to show visible progress in each area.

Figure 8 ▼

Student _____	Quarter: *1*
Course: *French II*	Date: *11/02/05*
Teacher: *Mrs. Yates*	Parent/Teacher Conference Suggested _____

Strengths/Accomplishments	**Evidence I will share**
- Writing in full sentences.	Homework paper - Speaking and sound studio
- Comprehending reading for young readers.	Classwork story - listening and viewing
- Make connections to cultural notes.	Free reading - reading logs
- Understanding stories that we read	Cultural notes - cultural
during class.	
Timed writes and making enough of an	
story so that I get a fairly good grade.	

Areas needing improvement	**A goal for next quarter**
Keeping my binder organized so that I	Work on timed writes at home to increase my
don't lose anything and have things so	vocab as well as writing. At least 4-5 by
that you can find them easily.	second quarter.

My Habits of Mind Self-Assessment:	Always	Usually	Sometimes	Rarely
I Have a Positive Attitude about Learning	✓			
I Demonstrate Perseverance	✓			
I Show Evidence of Quality Workmanship	✓			
I Show Evidence of Time Management	✓			

(Mt. Abram High School Self-Assessment of Learning)

The students needed to have evidence to back up their position on each of the five continua (Figure 8). They also needed an overall summary page of their strengths, evidence to share, areas to improve, a goal for the next quarter with an accompanying plan to achieve the goal, and a self-assessment section for "habits of mind" qualities. Each piece of evidence had a sticky note attached with the standard written on it, as well as a feeling/explanation about the work.

The conferencing took longer as the continua, evidence, and summary page were shared. The students and I discovered the continua needed some adjustments for clarity. The feedback from the students was incorporated into the five continua, which made the conferencing more comprehensive. It showed where each student was and where he or she wanted to go next in reading, writing, speaking, listening, and cultural connections. The students indicated the continua helped them to realize their abilities beyond looking at their grades or points. This step brings us closer to standards-based reporting.

The Journey Continues

At a recent TPRS training session, Blaine Ray talked about multi-level classes, the ultimate in non-tracking of students. The idea is to have a range of beginning through advanced students in the same class at the same time with the same curriculum. It is important *not* to shelter the structures of language, but instead shelter the vocabulary, just as when speaking to a baby. Babies acquire language because parents use repetitive phrases, all the tenses, and various language structures. In other words, it works to use the past tense right away, as well as the future; for example, "Here's a red ball. Catch the red ball. Oh, you caught the red ball! I'll throw the red ball again."

"Students suggested ways to better prove their learning…"

In the classroom, if the same principles are applied, students are challenged with "advanced" language structures while understanding more vocabulary as it is presented repetitively. As long as the curriculum changes every year, the upper level students will continue to be challenged. The curriculum could be repeated every four or five years, depending on the school. It has been tried with success at another high school in Colorado, with level one students expressing a feeling of frustration but learning more than those in the regular level one classroom. Blaine Ray suggested that care be taken not to lose the level one students; check in with them frequently for comprehension, be transparent with why and what is happening in the classroom, and have a wide variety of reading materials for all levels of readers.

While Blaine was explaining this concept, I kept thinking about how our small rural high school has a difficult time with scheduling, due to singleton classes: one or two French I and II classes, one French III and one French IV class. Historically, students could not always fit in a language class because of their schedule. The multi-level language class appealed to me as part of the solution to our scheduling nightmare. Nor would students be tracked, since all students could take any French class that fit into their schedule.

Our school approved the proposal to pilot several sections of "Uni-Français." We still have one French I and one French II class this year. The plan is to compare the pilot program with the traditional single level TPRS class at the end of the year. Our French students took the New York Regency Exam last spring and this year's students will also take the exam for comparison data. The students will be asked to reflect on their learning, as well as the multi-level approach, in order to implement improvements for next year. The multi-level approach is being piloted here in Salem, Maine, and in another location. The school in Colorado is continuing with multi-level classes for the second year due to the success they experienced in their pilot year.

"Their conferences focused more specifically on what they were learning and less on what grade they had."

We are into the second quarter of Uni-Français and the continua have helped to play a large part in assessment that seems appropriate for each student, regardless of how many years of French he or she may have taken. Language students thought about and decided where their skill level was on any given continuum standard, searched for evidence to back up their position, and set a goal for each standard for the following quarter.

Figure 9 ▼

Crystal L
French Quarter 2
Date January 19, 2006   Date: _____

Goals I have met:

Cultural	Reading	Writing	Speaking	Listening, Viewing
Identify and discuss connections between cultural values and socially approved behaviors of another culture	Jot down main ideas & supporting details	Write notes or short letters	Oral story sheets	Rosetta Stone lessons. Understand brief messages on familiar topics
Compare literature, art, or music from other culture with examples from own culture.	Weblog	Short stories	Speak clearly, make mistakes, but understandable	Understand class stories told by student or teacher
Cultural Connections log – info. gleaned from a variety of sources-compare and contrast	Textbooks, magazines, newspapers, non-fiction		Sing Songs	Evidence of listening skills

They *all* found a place for themselves on the continua. Their conferences focused more specifically on what they were learning and less on what grade they had or number of points on a quiz. Very few students used quizzes as evidence of their learning. Typically, they looked for work that could prove their depth of knowledge.

After only a year of using TPRS and student-based assessments, French II students are out performing the previous French IV "textbook style" students in writing and often in speaking Multi-level TPRS classes increased rigor in the curriculum, and the student-generated continua have resulted in gains in "ease of language" for the French I through level IV students. It appears to be most noticeable with the beginning students. As the journey of melding TPRS with assessment for learning continues, I am amazed at how willing most students are to try new approaches and to take a leadership role in their own learning.

For further information about *Teaching Proficiency through Reading and Storytelling,* go to www.blaineraytprs.com. There is a wealth of information and research at this site, sources of materials, and links to other TPRS-helpful sites.

References

Davies, A. (2000). *Making Classroom Assessment Work.* Courtenay, BC: Connections Publishing.

Gregory, K., C. Cameron, and A. Davies. (1997). *Knowing What Counts: Setting and Using Criteria.* Courtenay, BC: Connections Publishing.

Gregory, K., C. Cameron, and A. Davies. (2000). *Knowing What Counts: Self-Assessment and Goal-Setting.* Courtenay, BC: Connections Publishing.

Gregory, K., C. Cameron, and A. Davies. (2001). *Knowing What Counts: Conferencing and Reporting.* Courtenay, BC: Connections Publishing.

Gross, S. (2005). Developing Foreign Language Fluency. *International Journal of Foreign Language Teaching.* Vol 1(2), pp. 26, 27.

Rick Stiggins

Rick Stiggins, Ph.D., is founder and chief executive officer of the Assessment Training Institute of Portland Oregon. Since 1992, ATI's mission has been to support educators as they face the challenges of day-to-day classroom assessment. Most unique about their approach to assessment is ATI's advocacy of student involvement in the self-assessment, record keeping and communication process. This "assessment *for* learning" approach has yielded profound gains in student achievement through the effective management of the emotional dynamics of the assessment experience for learners. Rick's background includes a Ph.D. in educational measurement from Michigan State University, extensive experience in large-scale standardized testing, and decades of experience in creating and refining multimedia professional development experiences in assessment.

Redefining the Emotional Dynamics of Assessment

by Rick Stiggins

CONTENTS

Travel back to school in your mind's time machine. Your English teacher has just handed back your paper full of red corrections and a big red D, expressing frustration at your lack of achievement and threatening an F on your report card if you don't get going. Or, you're in middle school science class and your teacher startles everyone by instructing: "Take out a blank sheet of paper for a pop quiz." Or, you are in speech class and learn that your final speech will count for half of your grade. Or, your guidance counselor spells out in specific detail the dire consequences of college admissions test scores.

What do these scenarios have in common? They all reflect the belief among at least some of the teachers of our youth that the way to maximize motivation and, therefore, learning is to maximize the anxiety of the learner, and the intimidation of assessment is the way to do it. The more on edge students are, these teachers believed, the harder they will study and the more they will learn. To get more learning, demand it more vigorously; invoke the negative consequences of failure; use adult authority to hold students accountable for more learning; if a little intimidation doesn't work, turn up the heat with a lot of intimidation. These were familiar emotional dynamics of assessment for most of us during our schooling years. Essentially, the role of assessment was to perpetuate a constant state of fear. The key to effective schools was to scare students into learning.

Assessment as a Matter of Emotional Dynamics

This belief about the role of assessment merged neatly into the mission of the schools of our youth, which was to rank us from the highest to the lowest achiever by the end of high school. One function of schools was to begin to sort us into the various segments of our social and economic system. The amount of time available to learn was fixed: one year per grade. The amount learned by the end of that time was free to vary: some of us learned a great deal, some very little. Able learners built on past successes to grow rapidly. However, students who failed to master the early prerequisites within the allotted time failed to learn that which followed. After thirteen years of cumulative treatment in this manner, in effect, we were spread along an achievement continuum that literally labeled each student's rank in class upon graduation.

The emotional dynamics of this process were clear. From the very earliest grades, some students rode winning streaks. Right from the start, they scored high on assessments. The emotional effect of this was to help them come to believe themselves to be capable learners – they became increasingly confident in school. That gave them the emotional strength to risk striving for more success because in their minds, success was within reach if they tried. Notice, by the way, that the trigger for their learning success was *their interpretation of their own success* on assessments.

"Essentially, the role of assessment was to perpetuate a constant state of fear."

But other students scored very low on tests right from the beginning. This caused them to doubt their own capabilities as learners. They began to lose confidence which, in turn, deprived them of the emotional reserves to continue to risk trying. Chronic failure was hard to hide and became embarrassing. Better not to try. As their motivation waned, of course, achievement followed. Notice again how the learners' own interpretation of assessment results influenced their confidence and willingness to strive on.

In the schools of our youth, if some students worked hard and learned a lot, that was a positive result, as they would finish high in the rank order. And if some students gave up in hopeless failure, that was a necessary result too, because they would occupy places very low in the rank order. The greater the spread of achievement from top to bottom, the more dependable would be the rank order. This is why, if a student gave up and stopped trying (even dropped out of school), it was regarded as that student's problem, not the teacher's or school's. The school's responsibility was to provide the opportunity to learn. If students didn't take advantage of the opportunity, that was not the system's responsibility.

Some students respond to tougher academic challenges by working hard and learning, while others are driven to minimize their accumulating anxiety by escaping from the source; that is, by giving up in hopelessness. The result for the latter group? Exactly the opposite of the one society wants – they learn much less, not more. So, in effect, these intimidation-driven assessment practices have the effect of driving down the achievement of as many students as they have elevated; they have promoted as many losing streaks as winning streaks.

The important lesson we must learn is that the student's emotional reactions to assessment results will determine what the student thinks, feels, and does in response to those results. They can respond in either of two ways to any classroom or large-scale assessment, one productive and the other not. The productive reaction has students seeing the results and saying, "I understand these results. I know what to do next to learn more. I can handle this. I choose to keep trying." The counter-productive response leaves students saying, "I don't know what these results mean for me. I have no idea what to do next. I can't handle this. I quit."

If society wants all students to meet standards, then, as a pre-condition, all students must believe they can meet those standards; they all must be confident enough to be willing to take the risk of trying. Any other emotional state (such as the state of perpetual fear perpetrated in the schools of our youth) for any student is unacceptable. We can't have students who have yet to meet standards losing faith in themselves and giving up in hopelessness.

"The student's emotional reactions to assessment results will determine what the student thinks, feels, and does in response to those results."

As a society, over the past decade, we have come to understand that our ongoing and accelerating technical evolution and increasing ethnic diversity will demand citizens who are lifelong learners. We also have come to see that, in the above environment, students in the bottom third of the rank order, plus all who drop out without being ranked, fail to develop the foundational reading, writing, and math problem-solving proficiencies needed to function effectively in the future. As a result, society has asked its educators to raise the bottom of the rank order distribution to a certain level of achievement. We call these expectations our "academic achievement standards." Every state and province has them and, as a matter of public policy, schools are to be held accountable for making sure all students meet those standards.

Now, as a result, assessment practices that permitted, even encouraged, some students to give up on learning must be replaced by those that engender hope and sustained effort for all. In short, the entire emotional environment surrounding the experience of being evaluated must change, especially for perennial low achievers.

The driving emotional force of fear triggered by the prospect of an upcoming test must be replaced by confidence, optimism, and persistence – for all students, not just for some. All students must believe that, *"I can succeed at learning if I try."* They must have continuous access to credible evidence of their own academic success. This has spawned intense interest in "assessment *for* learning" – assessment used day-to-day by students and their teachers working together to maintain student confidence and to sustain learning success.

Assessments Must Inform the Learner Too

This emotional dimension of the student's assessment experience interacts directly with an associated intellectual dimension that is every bit as important as the emotional. The intellectual facet centers on the instructional decisions students make about their learning, based on their own interpretation of assessment results.

Over the decades, both school improvement experts and the measurement community have made the mistake of believing that the adults in the system are the most important assessment user/instructional decision-makers; that is, we have believed that, as the adults make better instructional decisions, schools will become more effective. Clearly parents, teachers, school leaders, and policy makers make crucial decisions that influence the quality of schools and the more data-based those decisions are, the better. But this discounts the fact that students may be even more important data-based instructional decision-makers than the adults.

"If a student decides that the learning is beyond reach for her or him or that the risk of public failure is too great and too humiliating, then regardless of what we adults do, there will be no learning."

Consider, for example, the reality that students are constantly deciding if they can do the learning. They ask, *"Can I get this stuff or am I just too dense? Is the learning worth the energy I must expend to attain it? Is the learning worth the risk of public failure?"* We must understand that, if students come down on the wrong side of these crucial decisions and thus stop trying, it doesn't matter what the adults around them decide. In effect, our students can render our instructional decisions null and void. They have it within their power to make us ineffective and to prevent us from doing anything about it. I don't mean that they would do so intentionally. But if a student decides that the learning is beyond reach for her or him or that the risk of public failure is too great and too humiliating, then regardless of what we adults do, there will be no learning.

So the essential issue for us adults is: *What can we do to help students answer the above questions in ways that keep them trying?*

We know how to do that, and it is not by intensifying the intimidation! Further, we know what will happen to student achievement when we put effective classroom assessment practices in place. Let me explain specifically what that means.

A Productive Dynamic: Classroom Assessment *for* Student Learning

Assessment *for* learning turns the classroom assessment process and its results into an instructional intervention designed to increase, not merely monitor, student learning. Research evidence gathered in hundreds of studies conducted, literally, around the world over the past decade (detailed on page 46), shows that the consistent application of principles of assessment *for* learning can give rise to unprecedented gains in student achievement, especially for perennial low achievers. The implications for such gains in raising test scores and closing achievement score gaps are profound.

To understand how these practices impact student learning, one must begin with a general sense of how assessment fits into instruction. We assess to draw inferences about student achievement for two reasons: to inform instructional decisions and to encourage students to try.

If assessment is, at least in part, the process of gathering evidence to inform instructional decisions, then the key starting questions for any assessment are: what decisions, who's making them, and what information will be helpful? In the case of assessment *for* learning, the key question is: *What comes next in the learning?* The key classroom decision-makers are teachers **and their students**. And, the information required centers on *where the student is now* in the progression of learning leading up to mastery of each academic achievement standard. The idea is never to leave students wondering where they are now, what success looks like and how to close the gap between the two. Students must never question *whether* they will succeed. Incremental success is always within reach.

Key Features and Roles

Perhaps the most unique feature of the assessment *for* learning process is that it acknowledges the critical importance of the instructional decisions made by students and their teachers, working as a team – it provides the information they need when they need it.

In that context, students become consumers of assessment information too, using evidence of their own progress to understand what comes next for them.

Another unique feature is its reliance on standards-based curriculum maps, written in easily understandable versions for teachers, students and family members, so that the trajectory (i.e., what has been learned and what comes next) is clear to all throughout the learning. This leads directly to our second reason for assessing: If we assess to motivate students to try, assessment for learning enables students by helping them watch themselves grow – by causing them to believe that success is within reach, if they keep trying.

Thus, it becomes clear that assessment *for* learning cannot happen just once a year or quarterly or even weekly. It must continue throughout the learning. To accomplish this, the teacher's classroom assessment role must play out in five parts:

"*Students must never question whether they will succeed. Incremental success is always within reach.*"

1. Become competent masters themselves of each of the standards their students are to master.

2. Understand how those standards transform into the curriculum that forms the scaffolding students will climb on their journey up to each standard.

3. Make those classroom-level achievement targets clear to students.

4. Transform the classroom targets into high-quality classroom. assessments, capable of accurately reflecting student achievement of those targets.

5. Use those assessments over time in collaboration with their students to inform key decisions and to help motivate students to keep learning.

One strategy teachers rely on in assessment *for* learning classrooms is to provide students with a *clear vision* of the learning target, from the beginning of the learning, along with *samples* of strong and weak work so they can see a progression to competence laid out before them. This builds confidence among learners by revealing the path to success. Another is to provide students with regular access to *descriptive* (versus evaluative or judgmental) feedback; that is, information that helps students understand how to improve the quality of their work. This requires repeated *self-assessments* so they can watch themselves successfully negotiating the road to competence. As students watch themselves succeeding, again, they become increasingly confident. Ultimately, students can learn to generate their own *descriptive feedback* (that is, learn to self-assess) and to *set goals* for what comes next in their learning. Each of these specific practices draws the learner more deeply into monitoring and taking responsibility for her or his own success.

Thus, the student's role in assessment *for* learning environments is to strive to understand what success looks like and to use each assessment to determine how to do better the next time. Assessments become more than one-time events attached onto the end of the teaching. They become part of the learning process by keeping students posted on their progress and confident enough to continue striving.

From Formative Assessment to Assessment *for* Learning

Assessment *for* learning is different from what historically has been referred to as "formative assessment." If formative assessment is about gathering evidence more frequently, assessment *for* learning is about gathering it continuously. If formative assessment is about teachers gathering and using evidence of learning, assessment *for* learning is about students gathering and using information about themselves too. If formative assessment tells users who is and is not meeting state standards, assessment *for* learning tells them what progress each student is making toward mastering each standard *while the learning is happening* – when there's still time to be helpful.

"Each of these specific practices draws the learner more deeply into monitoring and taking responsibility for her or his own success."

Assessment *for* learning is obviously different from summative assessment, which asks: *Which students have reached the top of the scaffolding?* These tests hold students and their teachers accountable for meeting required standards, as they should. They judge the sufficiency of learning at a particular point in time. State and district assessments, as well as classroom assessments for report card grading, represent examples of summative assessment.

In the perfect assessment system, one would seek to balance these various assessment purposes. The foundation would be a continuous array of assessments *for* learning used to help students learn more – to lead them along through increments of success. In addition, periodic early warning benchmark assessments would help teachers see student progress in terms of standards mastered, revealing to them who needs help with greater frequency than has been provided by once-a-year assessments. And finally, once-a-year accountability tests would rely on a variety of appropriate assessment formats (not merely multiple choice tests) to verify the ultimate level of student success. This balanced pattern promises to meet the information needs of all assessment users.

Research on Effects

When assessment *for* learning practices play out as a matter of routine in classrooms, as mentioned previously, evidence gathered around the world consistently reveals effect sizes of a half to one and a half standard deviations and more, directly attributable to the application of classroom assessment *for* learning. In his original mastery learning research, Bloom and his students (1984) made extensive use of classroom assessment in support of learning, in just the same terms as does the assessment *for* learning concept being described here, and reported subsequent gains in student test performance of one to two standard deviations. Black and Wiliam, in their 1998 watershed research review of over 250 studies from around the world on the impact of effective classroom assessment, reported gains of a half to a full standard deviation, with the largest gains being realized by low achievers. According to these researchers, the expected achievement score gains will rival in their impact on student achievement the implementation of one-on-one tutorial instruction, with the largest gains being realized by the lowest achievers, thus reducing achievement gaps.

But We Are Unprepared to Assess *for* Learning

"The risk of inaccurate classroom assessments remains high."

But the severe and chronic problem is that very few teachers and almost no school administrators have been given the opportunity to learn about principles of sound assessment practice of any sort, let alone assessment *for* learning. While virtually all licensing standards require competence in assessment, typically neither pre-service nor in-service teacher or administrator training programs include this kind of training (Crooks, 1989; Stiggins, 1999; Shepard, et al., 2005). As a result of this lack of preparation:

1. Educators are unable to differentiate among the various information needs of different assessment users, including students.

2. Achievement targets remain written at the state or district-level standards level rather than being translated into classroom-level learning progressions that lead up to each standard.

3. The risk of inaccurate classroom assessments remains high.

4. Feedback provided to students remains evaluative (such as grades) versus helpfully descriptive.

5. Students are rarely involved in self-assessment, tracking their own progress, or communicating their learning to others, all of which can give rise to profound learning gains.

The current state of affairs is clear: We know what teachers and administrators need to know and understand to assess effectively day-to-day in the classroom (Stiggins, Arter, Chappuis, and Chappuis, 2004). It is clear what will happen to student confidence, motivation and learning if they do so (see profound achievement gains reported on page 46). And we know how to deliver the proper classroom assessment competence into their hands with efficient and effective professional development (Stiggins and Chappuis, 2005). The only unanswered question is: *Will practitioners be given the opportunity to learn to assess for learning?* Historically, the answer has been an unequivocal, no. As a result, the immense potential of assessment *for* learning has gone untapped. It need not be so.

References

Black, P. & Wiliam, D. (1998). Assessment and classroom learning. *Educational Assessment: Principles, Policy and Practice,* 5(1), 7-74. Also summarized in an article entitled, Inside the black box: Raising standards through classroom assessment. *Phi Delta Kappan,* 80(2), 139-148.

Bloom, B. (1984). The search for methods of group instruction as effective as one-to-one tutoring. *Educational Leadership,* 41(8), 4-17.

Crooks, T.J. (1988). The impact of classroom evaluation on students. *Review of Educational Research,* 58(4), 438-481.

Shepard, L., Hammerness, K., Darling-Hammond, L., Rust, F., Snowden, J. B., Gordon, E., Gutierrez, C., & Pacheco, J. (2005) Chapter 8 in Darling-Hammond, L. & Bransford, J. (Eds) *Preparing teachers for a changing world: What teachers should know and be able to do.* San Francisco, CA: Jossey-Bass (note particularly pp. 282-284).

Stiggins, R.J. (1999). Evaluating classroom assessment training in teacher education. *Educational Measurement: Issues and Practice,* 18 (1), 23-27.

Stiggins, R.J., Arter, J., Chappuis, J., and Chappuis, S. (2004). *Classroom Assessment for Student Learning: Doing It Right – Using It Well.* Portland, OR: Assessment Training Institute.

Stiggins, R.J. and Chappuis, J. (2006) What a difference a word makes: Assessment *for* learning rather than assessment *of* learning helps students succeed. *Journal of Staff Development.* 27(1), 10-14.

Theme Two:
Learning Along with Students

Theme Two:
Learning Along with Students

Teachers learn along with their students as they use assessment *for* learning strategies. When students are engaged in setting criteria, self-assessing in relation to criteria, giving themselves and others specific, descriptive feedback, and receiving feedback, they learn more. When teachers examine and reflect on the work that students produce, they are giving themselves feedback about what worked for students and where needs have emerged. In Theme Two, teachers in different subject areas discuss how they and their students are shaping assessment *for* learning to produce evidence of achievement related to classroom, as well as system learning outcomes.

6   **Polly Wilson**, a biology teacher in Portland, Maine, works with students to set criteria for assignments, using samples to help them see the essential attributes of quality work in Science. She outlines how she developed ways to help students build and assess core knowledge and conceptual understandings, while giving non-graded feedback.

7   **Brent McKeown** and **Scott Horton**, English and Student Leadership teachers in Edmonton, Alberta, discuss the challenge of creating a meaningful classroom assessment system in the midst of system requirements – such as, final examinations marked centrally and worth 50% of a student's final grade. Success, in terms of student engagement and ownership, is signaled by students who ask questions such as, "What do I need to do to be able to demonstrate that I can achieve this course outcome?"

8   **Melissa J. Noack**, an Art teacher in Yarmouth, Maine, describes in detail how her students use protocols to give each other specific, descriptive feedback related to what needs to be learned and demonstrated in Fine Arts.

9   **Catherine A. Glaude**, High School Principal and Facilitator of School Improvement in Yarmouth, Maine, writes about using protocols to structure and guide conversations in ways that support adult learning and the learning of students.

10   Lastly, drawing on years of research as well as work at the National Writing Project (University of California, Berkeley), **Paul G. LeMahieu** and **Linda D. Friedrich** write about the importance of looking deeply at student work to create an assessment system that supports and improves student learning. They offer a practical process for classroom teachers to be engaged in developing an evaluative framework, through which their individual and joint judgments about student work can become fair, consistent and useful for accountability.

Polly Wilson

Polly Wilson, B.S., M.Ed., is fortunate to teach high school biology and marine ecology in Portland, Maine, where the ocean provides many teachable moments. She aspires to encourage her students in developing an appreciation for all creatures small and slimy. Currently, Polly is working to develop and field test curriculum that supports citizen science opportunities for students.

Assessments to Create the Foundations for Quality Work in Science Class

by Polly Wilson

What is quality work in science class? Is it essentially content-based? With the constant pressure to fit in content that seems to grow every year, how can teachers encourage students to look at their work and take the time to improve it? How can teachers find the time to teach students what quality work is without creating additional work for themselves? One way to address the overwhelming issues around analyzing quality work is to concentrate on a few obtainable goals, which can lend efficiency and focus to planning lessons and assessments.

There are two essential goals that I want my science students to reach: The first is an understanding of science concepts that is reflected by the correct use of science vocabulary. The second goal is for all students to be thorough and thoughtful in their work so that every assignment reflects their commitment to standards of quality. The challenge for me has been to incorporate assessments through which students could develop and present evidence that they have reached these goals. The assessments that I have found the most effective happily do not require a great deal of extra time on my part; instead they offer students an opportunity to compare their work to a standard and to apply what they have learned, in order to develop their understanding and to build strong connections. It is important for students to recognize value in what they are learning, so I want them to be able to connect science terms and concepts to real life situations, or to find instances where they can independently use something they learned earlier to make sense of something new.

Establishing and Using Criteria to Self-Assess

It is often difficult to maintain a minimum standard of quality for class work without putting a great deal of extra effort into correcting and grading. I have seen a significant difference in the quality of my students' work, without increasing my workload in terms of grading or scoring, by:

a)   establishing criteria
b)   making sure students understand how to fulfill the criteria
c)   expecting them to self-assess their work according to the criteria before handing it in

Criteria for General Assignments

In the past, my efforts at engaging students in enthusiastic and careful observations of what I considered to be fascinating pieces of the natural world consistently proved disappointing. Their observations were short, superficial and lacked the sense of wonder or curiosity I was hoping to foster. Devising questions to evoke more thought and information from the students proved equally disheartening, despite my instructions and encouragement. The seed of a solution was planted when I heard David Macauley, author of *The Way Things Work*, comment, "you truly see something when you draw it."

"…the criteria for a good drawing had to include attributes that were not about skill and talent but about completely representing the object."

In order for students to observe an object, they need to really look at it. Therefore, a complete drawing became the first step of any observation activity. Students generally discount their drawing ability and are apprehensive about putting pencil to paper. To alleviate their anxieties, the criteria for a good drawing had to include attributes that were not about skill and talent but about completely representing the object. The Criteria for a Good Drawing were designed around attributes such as "the size of the drawing must be large enough to show the essential components of the object, it must illustrate all the parts and show details about the features of the object, and it must also represent details such as textures and colors" (Figure 1). A book of nature sketches provided good examples of drawings of insects that, although simple, conveyed a large amount of information about the specimens. Those drawings made good exemplars with which to introduce the criteria.

In class, we talk about scale and how the parts of the specimen should represent their true size in relation to other parts, but since scale is often difficult for some to draw correctly, it is not on the list of basic criteria.

Figure 1 ▼

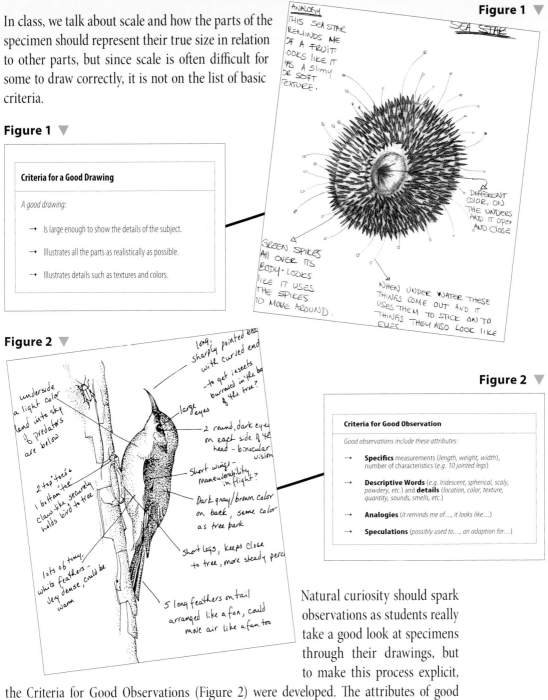

Criteria for a Good Drawing

A good drawing:

→ Is large enough to show the details of the subject.

→ Illustrates all the parts as realistically as possible.

→ Illustrates details such as textures and colors.

Figure 1 ▼

SEA STAR

ANALOGY
THIS SEA STAR REMINDS ME OF A FRUIT. OOKS LIKE IT HAS A SLIMY OR SOFT TEXTURE.

DIFFERENT COLOR, ON THE UNDERS AND IT OPEN AND CLOSE

GREEN SPIKES ALL OVER ITS BODY. LOOKS LIKE IT USES THE SPIKES TO MOVE AROUND.

WHEN UNDER WATER THESE THINGS COME OUT AND IT USES THEM TO STICK ON TO THINGS THEY ALSO LOOK LIKE EYES

Figure 2 ▼

long, sharply pointed beak with curved end
-to get insects in the bark burrowed in the bo of the tree?

underside a light color blend into sky if predators are below

large eyes

2 round, dark eyes on each side of the head - binocular vision

2 top toes + 1 bottom toe claw-like securely holds bird to tree

Short wings - maneuverability in flight?

Dark gray/brown color on back, same color as tree bark

lots of tiny, white feathers - very dense, could be warm

Short legs, keeps close to tree, more steady perch

5 long feathers on tail arranged like a fan, could move air like a fan too

Figure 2 ▼

Criteria for Good Observation

Good observations include these attributes:

→ **Specifics** measurements (*length, weight, width*), number of characteristics (*e.g. 10 jointed legs*)

→ **Descriptive Words** (*e.g. iridescent, spherical, scaly, powdery, etc.*) and **details** (*location, color, texture, quantity, sounds, smells, etc.*)

→ **Analogies** (*it reminds me of...., it looks like....*)

→ **Speculations** (*possibly used to...., an adaption for....*)

Natural curiosity should spark observations as students really take a good look at specimens through their drawings, but to make this process explicit, the Criteria for Good Observations (Figure 2) were developed. The attributes of good observations include quantitative specifics (for example, length, weight and width) and the use of descriptive words to convey an accurate picture of the specimen. For example, a student with special needs created the illustration shown in Figure 3 and used the criteria to shape her written observation:

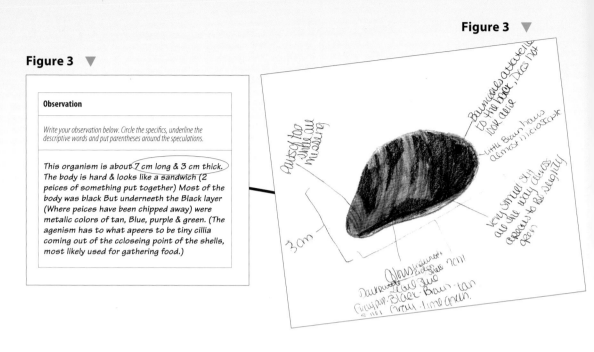

Figure 3 ▼

Figure 3 ▼

Observation

Write your observation below. Circle the specifics, underline the descriptive words and put parentheses around the speculations.

This organism is about 7 cm long & 3 cm thick. The body is hard & looks like a sandwich (2 peices of something put together) Most of the body was black But underneeth the Black layer (Where peices have been chipped away) were metalic colors of tan, Blue, purple & green. (The agenism has to what apeers to be tiny cillia coming out of the ccloseing point of the shells, most likely used for gathering food.)

Stretching Student Inquiry

As an introduction, it is both fun and useful to have students examine something while blindfolded and offer a description, to demonstrate how to use senses other than sight to gather information. Analogy and speculation are also included as attributes of a good observation to encourage higher-level thinking and making connections to prior knowledge. These attributes also help students to build new knowledge from what they already know and can encourage further research. Printed on the back of the criteria handout is an example of a drawing with observation attributes written around it to serve as an example for students.

Figure 4 ▼

Observations Include:	Feedback	Current Score
Descriptive Details		
Analogies		
Speculations		

Make improvements in a different color ink and hand in for a grade.

To support students as they apply basic observation criteria, I also give feedback related to each of the criteria on early assignments. This provides opportunities for them to refine and improve their work before it is graded. Figure 4 is a sample feedback sheet.

Adding Criteria

Figure 5 ▼

The wide variety in the quality of answers provided by students on various activities and assignments indicated a need for developing Criteria for Thorough Answers (Figure 5). With the implementation of these criteria, it became clearer to students that details and supporting information were expected in a thoroughly answered question. Since many of them believe that a thorough answer equals a wordy answer, the criteria handout includes four examples of various answers to help dispel this confusion. Students are asked to read the answers and to score them using the rubric. Most will be able to recognize one of the answers as having many words but little substance. Reviewing the scores to these answers with the class can provoke a discussion to underscore the distinction between *thorough* and *wordy*.

These basic criteria are introduced at the beginning of the course and serve as expectations for quality work in science class throughout the course. Students are expected to keep the criteria lists handy

Thorough Answers Include:

→ First sentence provides the basic answer.
→ Subsequent sentences provide supporting information such as:
  → Details
  → Explanations
  → Examples

3	2	1
Correct answer with supporting information	Correct answer without adequate support	Provides too little information to show knowledge

Figure 6 ▼

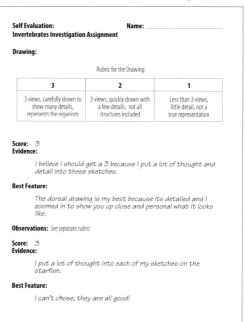

Self Evaluation:
Invertebrates Investigation Assignment   Name: _____

Drawing:

Rubric for the Drawing

3	2	1
3 views, carefully drawn to show many details, represents the organism	3 views, quickly drawn with a few details, not all structures included	Less than 3 views, little detail, not a true representation

Score: 3
Evidence:
I believe I should get a 3 because I put a lot of thought and detail into these sketches.

Best Feature:
The dorsal drawing is my best because its detailed and I zoomed in to show you up close and personal what it looks like.

Observations: *See separate rubric*

Score: 3
Evidence:
I put a lot of thought into each of my sketches on the starfish.

Best Feature:
I can't chose, they are all good!

Figure 6 ▼

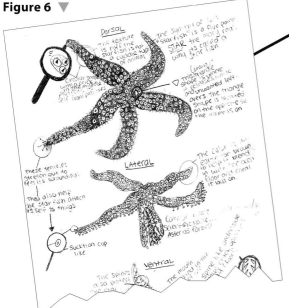

as a reference for the entire semester. In order to encourage the habit of self-assessment, early inquiry activities include handouts that require students to formally self-assess their work according to the criteria. In addition to the actual criteria, I use self-assessment activities to reinforce for my students the need for them to be able to point out evidence of their learning. An example is shown in Figure 6. Formal self-assessment is not required in later assignments, but as the semester continues, I remind students not to hand in work until it meets the established criteria. If it doesn't, the student is asked to compare the work to the criteria and make the necessary adjustments before handing it in. Along with the basic criteria, I also require students to show content mastery and conceptual understanding.

Figure 7 ▼

Water Chemistry – The Properties of Water

"The most important thing about the ocean is that it is full of water."
                                                    -Henry Bryant Bigelow

On the 11x17 paper provided, create a chart that organizes all of the information you will need to respond to Bigelow's quote.

The chart should have 3 columns:

Label		How to fill in the information
The Property of water	▸	List one of the 4 properties we learned.
The molecular structure and functions that cause the property	▸	Don't just say polarity! Explain exactly what is happening with the molecules to create the property.
How the property affects environments and living things	▸	Describe, not list, many examples.

The chart should have a row for each of the 4 properties of water that we have learned. Like this – only much larger.

Property	The Molecular Structure...	How the property affects...
#1 stickiness		
#2 heat capacity		
#3 density		
#4 universal solvent		

Criteria for Specific Assignments

There are two key criteria that cut across many different assignments:

- Core knowledge
- Conceptual understanding

Building and Assessing Core Knowledge

Some assignments are designed to make sure students are aware of and address the *knowledge* at the heart of a particular scientific concept. Others require students to compile and organize information necessary for them to move to the next level of conceptual understanding. In developing and organizing assignment criteria, I consider what information and connections are the most valuable in helping students to learn science concepts.

Two examples of this are the Water Chemistry and the Energy in Ecosystems assignments. Both give students the opportunity to organize and to make sense of information they have learned in class. The first one helps students organize their knowledge of water chemistry in order to respond to a quote that will serve as the unit test. Figure 7 shows scaffolding that I provide for students as they gather and begin to organize information.

The Water Chemistry assignment is focused on two main points I expect students to address competently on the test: The Molecular Structure and Functions that Cause the Properties (of water) and How the Property Affects Environments and Living Things (Figure 8).

Creating a comparison chart is a common activity in this and other assignments, but in this case, I want students to be very aware of how organizing information helps to prepare them to speak about that information on a more sophisticated level. Students self-assess their work and then think about how prepared they are to show their understanding on the test.

Figure 8 ▼

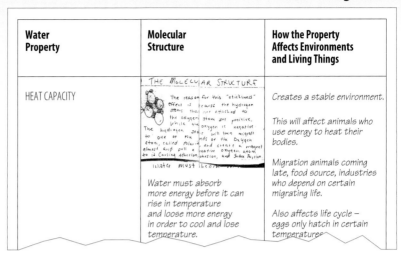

Water Property	Molecular Structure	How the Property Affects Environments and Living Things
HEAT CAPACITY	THE MOLECULAR STRUCTURE The reason for this "stickiness" effect is because the hydrogen atoms that are attached to the oxygen atom are positive, while the oxygen is negative. The hydrogen atom will then migrate to one of two ends of the oxygen atom, called polarity, and create a magnet almost and pull a negative oxygen atom to it causing adhesion, cohesion, and surface tension. Water must absorb more energy before it can rise in temperature and loose more energy in order to cool and lose temperature.	Creates a stable environment. This will affect animals who use energy to heat their bodies. Migration animals coming late, food source, industries who depend on certain migrating life. Also affects life cycle – eggs only hatch in certain temperatures.

Building and Assessing Conceptual Understanding Assignments

The Energy in Ecosystems assignment requires students to organize and *connect* (diagram and explain) a great deal of information. Since this assignment is fairly complicated, the criteria are structured and clarified as detailed lists of information to include and connect.

Figure 9 ▼

Energy in Ecosystems

Concept: Understands the movement of energy through ecosystems

Task: Create a diagram that details the movement of energy through an ecosystem and explain the processes that are involved.

Criteria details:
Trophic Levels
→ Show 4 trophic levels and decomposers
→ Show biodiversity by representing each tropic level with multiple species...
→ Indicate the common and scientific name of each species
→ ....

Energy Transfer
→ Indicate the shifting, use and dispersal of energy within each tropic level...
→ ...

Processes....

Figure 9 ▼

the first trophic level, not much of that energy makes to the top consumer. For example, for every 10 units of energy generated by the producers only .01 units of that energy makes it to the top trophic level

Canadian Goose - Branta

At every level, some of the energy is lost to decomposers (bacteria, fungi) who re filter the energy through waste

Secondary Consumers

energy

Stickleback - Gasterosteus

Killfish - Fundulus

American Eel - Anguilla

Primary Consumers
this level gets its energy when it consumes the plants

mussle - Geukensia

Sponge - Porifera

clam -

energy

heat

Students self-assess on the basis of including all of the required information and considering how their work shows evidence of understanding energy transfer. Subsequent activities help students to acquire even more in-depth understanding of this key concept. Figure 9 is an excerpt from the task and criteria sheet for this assignment.

Connections Across Content

Teachers look at the bigger picture of science knowledge and carefully plan lessons and units based on sequences of information to maximize student understanding. Concept A is taught before concept B so that the information from A will provide a foundation for B, but students often appear to view each lesson or unit as independent from other topics. You can imagine students locking the door on a unit after the test is completed and throwing away the key. When students are asked to make explicit connections from one topic to the next, it asks them to think harder and more broadly. In my classes, I use two strategies to help students make connections.

Putting our Work into Perspective

Figure 10 ▼

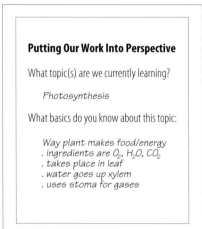

> **Putting Our Work Into Perspective**
>
> What topic(s) are we currently learning?
>
>   *Photosynthesis*
>
> What basics do you know about this topic:
>
>   *Way plant makes food/energy*
>   *. ingredients are O_2, H_2O, CO_2*
>   *. takes place in leaf*
>   *. water goes up xylem*
>   *. uses stoma for gases*

The Putting our Work in Perspective activity was designed to combat this tunnel vision. It asks students to identify what they are currently learning in science class, explain some of what they know about that topic and connect the current topic to previous topics that were already covered. When introducing this activity for the first time, the class compiles a list of previous topics to job their memories and provide them with the information necessary to begin to form connections. I also model a connection so they are clear about the expectaions. The Criteria for a Thorough Answer might also be followed to guide the quality of answers in this activity. The Putting our Work in Perspective format can be tweaked in many ways and has proven to be a very useful assessment tool when used alone or when attached to a specific assignment, such as a drawing that illustrates the basics of photosynthesis (Figure 11).

Figure 11 ▼

Figure 11 ▼

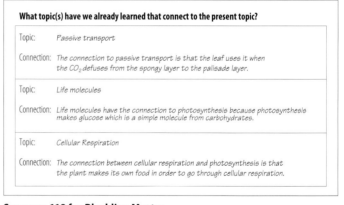

Connections

The 3 connections in this project that connects to previous knowledge are:

Passive Transport: *Photosynthesis uses Passive Transport because when the CO_2 goes from the spongey layer to the Palisade layer it uses no energy to defuse.*

Life Molecules: *Photosynthesis has a connection to life molecules because photosynthesis creates glucose which is a simple molecule created by starches.*

Cellular Respiration: *Photosynthesis has a connection to cellular respiration because it makes its own food so that it can go through cellular respiration.*

In the first section, students describe what they are currently learning. The second section provides space for the connections students are asked to make. These connections are often very enlightening and valuable in assessing what students comprehend.

Figure 12 ▼

These four questions, which I use repeatedly in my classes, have proved to strengthen student learning:

1. *What is it (the current topic)?*
2. *Why is it important?*
3. *What does it look like?*
4. *What if there wasn't any?*

What topic(s) have we already learned that connect to the present topic?

Topic:	*Passive transport*
Connection:	*The connection to passive transport is that the leaf uses it when the CO_2 defuses from the spongy layer to the palisade layer.*
Topic:	*Life molecules*
Connection:	*Life molecules have the connection to photosynthesis because photosynthesis makes glucose which is a simple molecule from carbohydrates.*
Topic:	*Cellular Respiration*
Connection:	*The connection between cellular respiration and photosynthesis is that the plant makes its own food in order to go through cellular respiration.*

See page 118 for Blackline Master

In order to answer these simple questions, students have to pull that science concept from its lofty perch and describe it as they might to a younger sibling who asks, *"What is it?"* This process helps students solidify their understandings.

Try This Out: Ask groups of three or four students to build answers to these questions around any topic or concept and present their ideas to the class. This exercise sparks a great deal of meaningful discussion and exchange within the groups and often creates the moment where students finally *get it*.

When students provide feedback regarding activities that are helpful to increasing their understanding, this exercise is consistently cited. I find that guiding students through the process of building upon previous knowledge does improve the overall quality of thinking in science class, and I am hopeful that students will repeat the practice in other venues.

Cooperative Concept Mapping

Another powerful and effective formative assessment that promotes connections, yet doesn't require grading, is cooperative concept mapping. Groups of three or four students are given handouts with a list of relevant vocabulary words and a large blank sheet of paper. The group is instructed to cut the words out of the handout and arrange them in such a way as to demonstrate their understanding of a concept. Actually manipulating the cutout words as if they were a puzzle seems to involve students in a way that simple reading or writing does not. The teacher can move among the groups and ask questions to spark ideas. When a group feels they have arranged the words to demonstrate a correct understanding of the concept (groups often come up with different, but correct arrangements) they explain their work to the teacher. Sometimes students draw arrows to make their ideas clear. When their concept map is complete, they glue the words in place and post their work. Usually one or two of the groups then present their ideas to the class. Students are encouraged to copy a map to keep in their study notes.

Figure 13 ▼

Criteria	In Progress	Finished Product
Completion ___ Fish Biology ___ Fishery Info ___ Management ideas	Looks good: · Work on:	
Connections to fish biology	Looks good: Work on:	
Thoroughness of descriptions of management ideas	Looks good: Work on:	
Own words		

See page 119 for Blackline Master

Non-Graded Feedback

Non-graded feedback informs students of their progress as they work on an assignment. Non-graded feedback might be offered by peers or by the teacher. Its purpose is to help students understand what is good about their work and to identify areas that need improvement. It should serve to improve the level of work that is handed in.

Feedback Sheets

Student research projects are good examples of assignments whose quality can be improved by non-graded feedback. The Fisheries Research and Management Plan Feedback sheet (see figure 13) provides an example of a very specific non-graded feedback form that allows peers to contribute their feedback. It can also be used by the students themselves as a self-assessment tool or by the teacher. The final column, labeled Finished Product, is where the teacher makes comments when grading the piece.

I often use non-graded feedback on lab report conclusions because students tend to treat a conclusion as a quick review of a lab rather than the opportunity to connect the data they gathered with the concept the lab demonstrates. The criteria for a good conclusion to a lab report involve three basic parts:

1. identifying the purpose of the lab

2. demonstrating an understanding of the science concept illustrated by the lab

3. explaining how the data gathered in the lab supports or refutes the concept.

The From Corn to Milk (Figure 14) lab is an example of how students are asked to organize a conclusion according to the criteria and includes student work from a sophomore biology class.

Figure 14 ▼

> Conclusion:
>
> The purpose of the lab was to be able to identify any similarities in the life molecules that are in corn and the life molecules that are in milk and say why the molecules in corn might be similar to the ones in milk.
>
> Feedback:
>
> Paragraph 1: Good extra part about the "why" of the lab
>
> Finally you now know that everything use is life molucles because even the smallest things like corn and cheese give off lipids and you alread know that lipids store energy, and that is what is a life molicule I guess.
>
> Your last paragraph of this section is good, but can you make it more specific? Instead of the word "everything" use details. Don't put "I guess" in a report. Please redo this so that it is talking about corn (plants) and milk (animal products). Check your spelling and grammar.

Figure 15 ▼

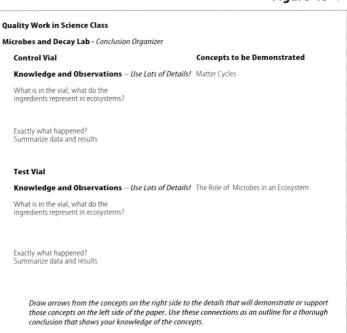

Quality Work in Science Class

Microbes and Decay Lab - *Conclusion Organizer*

Control Vial   **Concepts to be Demonstrated**

Knowledge and Observations — *Use Lots of Details!* Matter Cycles

What is in the vial, what do the ingredients represent in ecosystems?

Exactly what happened?
Summarize data and results

Test Vial

Knowledge and Observations — *Use Lots of Details!* The Role of Microbes in an Ecosystem

What is in the vial, what do the ingredients represent in ecosystems?

Exactly what happened?
Summarize data and results

Draw arrows from the concepts on the right side to the details that will demonstrate or support those concepts on the left side of the paper. Use these connections as an outline for a thorough conclusion that shows your knowledge of the concepts.

Charts

With labs that occur early in the course or with complicated labs, it is invaluable to help students organize the information needed to satisfy the three criteria on charts. Figure 15 is an example of a chart that facilitates the organization of material for a microbe lab.

First Drafts

To ensure that students are making sense of a lab, I usually collect the first drafts of lab conclusions and offer non-graded feedback to guide their work on a final draft. It is helpful to require students to include the first draft and its non-graded feedback with their final lab report to check and see if the feedback and subsequent revision really helped move the student toward greater understanding. It is important to note that a few students do not act upon the feedback and will turn in unimproved work. I will **not** accept this work as a completed assignment. The extra step of non-graded feedback appears to add more effort to the grading of lab reports, an already labor-intensive activity for science teachers, but because comparisons to the first draft can easily be made, the grading process proceeds very quickly.

"…a few students do not act upon the feedback and will turn in unimproved work. I will not accept this work as a completed assignment."

Quick Fixes

An on-the-spot version of non-graded feedback is what I call a *quick fix*. Quick fixes serve to encourage the habit of making improvements to what students might already consider finished work. Students are directed to use a different colored pencil or pen from the one they originally used to complete their assignment and make any corrections that are necessary for all of the information in their work to be correct and complete. The improvements are made as we go over the assignment in class and students are able to compare what they have done with the correct answers or information. The assignments that can be quick fixed are most often homework or short class work that is scored with a minus, a check or a plus. Students receive a plus if their work shows that they made a good or excellent attempt the first time and took advantage (if needed) of the opportunity to improve their work further. Quick fixes engage students as we go over assignments, and help them to identify information that can improve their work.

Conferences

One of the most powerful means of self-assessment and reflection is for students to speak directly to their parents about their learning and progress in school. Since student-led conferences are not standard practice in many high schools, it is important to develop ways to bring the student's voice to parent-teacher conferences. The student, after all, is the largest stakeholder in their own education, so it is important to encourage student involvement. The Conference Preparation Questions (Figure 16) were devised to offer an opportunity for students to reflect upon their progress in class, their strengths in general and what future actions they may take to improve their education in a way that is constructive and informative for parents, teachers and students. The questions were formed to eliminate the tendency of focusing conferences solely on grades.

Class time is allocated for every student to complete the questionnaire, regardless of whether his or her parent will schedule a conference. Their responses provide very valuable feedback. Here are 3 examples:

Describe your strengths in this class and at school in general

"We often think every assessment must be graded or scored, but that's not so."

- *My strengths are labs, I'm pretty good at those. I'm also really good at learning the material.*

Describe your level of involvement and your contributions when participating in group assignments.

- *When we do group assignments I try and make sure no one is left out and everyone is participating.*

Can you identify any actions (improve study habits, participation, etc.) that will help you to be more successful in class?

- *I will need to improve on my studying habits. I want to get better and better and not procrastinate on projects or assignments.*

Ideally the student presents his or her responses to the Conference Preparation Questions in person at a table around which their parents and teacher are also gathered. Usually a third of my students participate. Students can also conference with me directly if their parents do not schedule a meeting. The students use their conference script so they are not at a loss for words. The responses often spark conversations between all the parties

Figure 16 ▼

See page 120 for Blackline Master

present. Six years of inviting students to participate in conferences have resulted in only positive experiences.

Since my school conferences do not receive one hundred percent participation and students are not required to attend, I will also conduct the conference around the student's answers even though the student is not present. Parents appreciate learning what their son or daughter believes is important in regards to succeeding in class and school.

Conclusion

It is important that assessments designed to improve student learning and the quality of student work be practical and efficient. We often think every assessment must be graded or scored, but that's not so. Assessments *for* learning are *tools* to help students learn and should provide an opportunity for teachers to see if their students are on the right track before a test is taken. Students need to know how to identify the quality in their own work and to add what is needed to earn a high grade. They need to understand how to build knowledge from the tools and information that surround them at school but are often unnoticed or not apparent. Thoughtful and effective assessments help students understand the strategies necessary to learn, to show their learning, and to succeed.

References

Education Development Center. (1998). *Insights in Biology: The Matter of Life Manual.* Dubuque, IA: Kendall/Hunt Publishing Co. (Inspired the Corn to Milk Lab.)

Leslie, C.W. (1995). *Nature Drawing: A Tool for Learning.* Dubuque, IA: Kendall/Hunt Publishing Co.

Microbial Literacy Collaborative (Community Outreach Initiative). (1999). *Meet the Microbes through the Microbe World Activities: Now You See it, Now You Don't.* Reston, VA: National Association of Biology Teachers. (Inspired the Microbe and Decay Lab.)

Brent McKeown, B.A., B.Ed., is the English Department Head at Harry Ainlay High School in Edmonton, Alberta.

Brent McKeown & Scott Horton

Brent and Scott undertook the work described in this chapter while they were colleagues in the English Department at M.E. Lazerte High School. They continue their collaborative efforts in teaching, assessment and writing and have devoted much of their recent energies to sharing their ideas, techniques and experiences with colleagues throughout North America, by way of formal conference presentations and informal discussions.

Scott Horton, B.Ed., is the Department Head of Student Leadership at Ross Sheppard High School in Edmonton, Alberta.

Reading Our Students: A Foundation for Meaningful Assessment

by Brent McKeown and Scott Horton

"Do not dictate to your author; try to become him. Be his fellow-worker and accomplice. If you hang back, and reserve and criticize at first, you are preventing yourself from getting the fullest possible value from what you read. But if you open your mind as widely as possible, then signs and hints of almost imperceptible fineness, from the twist and turn of the first sentences, will bring you into the presence of a human being unlike any other."

Virginia Woolf, *How Should One Read a Book*

Consider a possible paraphrase of Woolf's famous words:

> Do not dictate to your *student*; try to become him. Be her fellow-worker and accomplice. If you hang back, and reserve and criticize at first, you are preventing yourself from getting the fullest possible *potential* from *your student*. But if you open your mind as widely as possible, then signs and hints of almost imperceptible fineness, from the twist and turn of the *first lessons*, will bring you into the presence of a human being unlike any other.

This re-envisioning of Woolf's famous words will be familiar to any teacher who has struggled with the contradictions inherent to teaching within an assessment framework that is too narrow to appreciate the complexities of the learning process. As two English teachers in large urban high schools who engage with students and the system through multiple roles, including departmental leadership, we are afforded the opportunity to speak with students about the different ways that English is presented to them. Too often these conversations have been extremely disheartening. Students equate English class with work sheets and study guides rather than with a genuine love for language and literature.

This is our story and it is a story born of a profound personal and professional need. We are both teachers who are passionate about our subject and our students, yet for all the professional success and personal satisfaction that our jobs have brought us, there always seemed to be something missing. That "something" was an assessment framework that fit with our professional ideals about what it means to be a teacher. Too often we found ourselves in situations where so much of the good work that we did in the classroom was at odds with the often rigid and short-sighted assessment systems that we, and so many of our colleagues, felt chained to. But if there were chains, they were really only chains of our own devices, locked through our lack of courage and conviction. We set out to change things by devising an assessment system that spoke to our students and ourselves in a meaningful and deeply personal way. We want to share our story, because we believe that ultimately it is up to teachers to use their own professional autonomy to make meaningful change at the classroom level.

"The basic premise behind our assessment system is a simple one: to balance the achievement of the specific course outcomes...with a genuine love of learning, language and literature."

This has been the most exhilarating, and exhausting year of our professional careers. Surprisingly, the process itself became our most powerful teaching tool, and our students soon recognized that they were in the midst of a living, breathing research project. Having identified the need for a meaningful assessment system, we set out to devise a learning structure which reflected our core values and goals, including a transparent and involved process for our students and ourselves. The year included moments of genuine inspiration as well as wandering down some dark alleys. Our students saw us struggling with assessment on a day-to-day basis and they, too, were actively engaged in these struggles. What follows is a brief summary of the process we engaged in, as well as the basic components of the assessment system we devised.

Beginnings

In early August of 2004, we spent the better part of two days sitting in a classroom grappling with the fundamental questions regarding what we need and want from an assessment system. We talked about some of our frustrations with systems we had used in the past; namely, attempting to reconcile an outcome and skill-based curriculum with the too common practice of simply adding up marks to communicate student learning – a practice that seems to punish students for lack of skill early on and does not allow for the recognition of the vast growth over the course of a semester. We reflected on some of the ideals that we had explored through our own reading and research on assessment, going back to our pre-professional years. At the end of these two days we came up with a basic framework to serve as our starting point for all of our classes. We were also scheduled to team-teach two Grade Eleven International Baccalaureate (IB) English classes and we viewed our experience with these classes as being the cornerstone of our structure.

Figure 1 ▼

The basic premise behind our assessment system is a simple one: to balance the achievement of the specific course outcomes, the most fundamental purpose of any course, with a genuine love of learning, language and literature. The Alberta provincial government provides us with detailed documents, built around five General Learner Outcomes that actually state exit outcomes for the course (Figure 1). These guide us in planning ways to help our students demonstrate their ability to achieve these course outcomes, hopefully at veryhigh levels. There are three major components to our course structure: Windows, Foundations, and Projects.

Curricular Outcomes

Every English course at the high school level is constructed around the following five general learner outcomes:

Students will listen, speak, read, write, view and represent to . . .

General Outcome #1   Explore thoughts, ideas, feelings and experiences.

General Outcome #2   Comprehend literature and other texts in oral, print, visual and multi media forms, and respond personally, critcially and creatively.

General Outcome #3   Manage ideas and information.

General Outcome #4   Create oral, print, visual and multimedia texts, and enhance the clarity and artistry of communication.

General Outcome #5   Respect, support and collaborate with others.

Component 1: Windows

The Windows assignments are designed to allow students the opportunity to enjoy a meaningful and engaging culminating learning task at regular intervals in the course. Approximately every five to seven classes, our students would do a Windows assignment that reflects the ideas and skill sets they have been developing over the previous two to three weeks. Why call them *Windows?* (This is actually a question that we ask all of our students in our course outlines and some of them have even done a Windows assignment where they explore the nature of Windows.) As a metaphor for some of the tasks that we do in an English class, think of this: If you look outside a window during the day you will see a clear picture of what is outside, but if you keep standing there until the sun goes down, eventually the window starts turning into a mirror. That combination of looking

Figure 2 ▼

EFFECTIVE COMMUNICATION

5 Evidence chosen to support ideas is consistently convincing and works to strengthen the overall impression. There is a consistently seamless connection between the intended purpose and the choice of form. The student demonstrates advanced ability to control a range of forms. The intended purpose is consistently clearly communicated.

4 Evidence chosen to support ideas is consistently convincing and works to strengthen the overall impression. There is a consistently strong connection between the intended purpose and the choice of form. The student demonstrates the ability to control a range of forms. The intended purpose is consistently clearly communicated.

MEANINGFUL PRODUCT

5 Consistently insightful exploration of the given topics. Assignments consistently represent a culmination of the work and strategies used in prior classes. The student has engaged in independent inquiry beyond the confines of the classroom. The student clearly demonstrates that the completed assignments and the creation process itself are meaningful both to the student and the audience.

4 Consistently thoughtful exploration of the given topics. Assignments consistently represent a culmination of the work and strategies used in prior classes. The student has engaged in independent inquiry beyond the confines of the classroom. The student shows an understanding of how process and product can be meaningful both to the student and the audience.

ENGLISH 20IB
WINDOWS REFLECTIONS

Please take a few moments to read the comments and marks that your team has written on your first four Windows assignments. Check off each assignment as you read the comments.and offer a self-assessment using the Windows Rubric.

#1 _____
#2 _____
#3 _____
#4 _____

a) Based on the feedback you have received, list at least two things that you think you have done well on your Windows assignments so far.

1.

2.

b) Based on the feedback you have received, list at least two things that you think you could improve on in future Windows assignments.

1.

2.

Based on the feedback you have received and using the Windows Marking Rubric as a guide, how do you think you are doing overall on your Windows Assignments:

Meaningful Product	1	2	3	4	5
Effective Communication	1	2	3	4	5
Rationale:					

---

in and looking out speaks to what we hope our students will experience with every assignment, project, activity and discussion within this assessment framework.

These assignments take various forms, but they characteristically feature two or three parts to them. Typically, students will be asked to complete these assignments in a week's time, although there may be times when the depth and complexity of the assignment requires more or less time. They are essentially culminating minor assignments that provide a regular answer to the question: How do we know what our students have learned?

Students receive feedback in various ways depending on the nature of the assignment. In some cases we use existing common rubrics for the Personal and Critical writing assignments established by the government. Sometimes we design task-specific rubrics and include commentary on specific areas of the assignment. Ultimately, however, we offer a holistic assessment of how each student is progressing in their Windows assignments, and for this we developed a *Windows*-specific rubric based on the needs of our classroom, as mandated by the provincial curriculum. We do these assessments just prior to each reporting period, so that the marks represent the most recent progress made by the student in these assignments. Our teacher assessments are preceded by the students' self-assessments, which allow them the opportunity to actively reflect upon their own learning processes.

Component 2: The Foundations Workshop

The Foundations Workshop was designed as a way to address the powerful learning moments in our classrooms that often are not reflected in the transition from student performance to a number grade. While building on both the general and specific provincial course outcomes, we attempted to refine them in such a way that we – as well as students and parents – can look at learning progress in discreet areas of the course.

Figure 3a ▼

> **FOUNDATIONS WORKSHOP: Assessment Guide**
>
> **MEANINGFUL PROGRESS**
>
> **5** The student provides tangible evidence of achievement of this group of course outcomes consistent with the current stage of the course and the student's own individual developmental needs and goals. At this point in the course the student has clearly demonstrated the ability to achieve these outcomes at **consistently high levels of thought and process.** The student demonstrates the ability to engage with language and literature using **a wide range of strategies – including the various relevant strands of the language arts-** that speak to immediate, practical concerns, while also emphasizing a sense of **commitment to lifelong learning.** The student has **consistently demonstrated an advanced understanding** of his/her own thinking and learning processes. **The student demonstrates extremely strong abilities in this outcome area.**
>
> **4** The student provides tangible evidence of achievement of this group of course outcomes consistent with the current stage of the course and the student's own individual developmental needs and goals. At this point in the course the student has clearly demonstrated the ability to achieve these outcomes **at frequently high levels of thought and process.** The student demonstrates the ability to engage with language and literature using **a range of strategies – including the various relevant strands of the language arts-** that speak to immediate, practical concerns, while also emphasizing a sense of **commitment to lifelong learning.** The student has **frequently demonstrated an effective understanding** of his/her own thinking and learning processes. **The student demonstrates strong abilities in this outcome area.**

5a. Respect and Appreciate Others

Meaningful Progress   1   2   3   4   5   NA

Rationale:

5b. Working With a Group

Meaningful Progress   1   2   3

Rationale:

OTHER COMMENTS:

3b. Assess Information/Form

Meaningful Progress   1   2   3   4   5   NA

Rationale:

4a. Development of Print and Non-Print Text

Meaningful Progress   1   2   3

Rationale:

4b. Develop Content and Consider Context

Meaningful Progress   1   2   3

Rationale:

4c. Improve Thoughtfulness, Effectiveness a

Meaningful Progress   1   2   3

Rationale:

2b. Use Reference Strategies

Meaningful Progress   1   2   3

Rationale:

2c. Understanding and Appreciation

Meaningful Progress   1   2   3

Rationale:

2d. Positions and Issues

Meaningful Progress   1   2   3

Rationale:

3a. Plan Inquiry and Research

Meaningful Progress   1   2   3

Rationale:

Figure 3b ▼

FOUNDATIONS REFLECTIONS

Using the Foundations Rubric as your guide, please offer a self assessment regarding your progress in each of the Foundations areas. Please offer a brief rationale after each assessment. In your rationale you could simply list or comment upon the work that you have done that supports the Meaningful Progress mark you have circled.

1a. Strategies for Learning

Meaningful Progress   1   2   3   4   5   NA

Rationale:

1b. Personal Understandings

Meaningful Progress   1   2   3   4   5   NA

Rationale:

2a. Understanding Content and Context

Meaningful Progress   1   2   3   4   5   NA

Rationale:

The Foundations Workshop takes the initial form of a tracking sheet in which students track their own progress in each of these areas, while we do the same.

Figure 4 ▼

At regular intervals, as with the Windows, we offer a holistic assessment based on the student's progress in each of these areas. Again, we ask students to engage in a self-assessment prior to our assessment and evaluation.

In the last stage of the course, the Foundations Workshop evolves into a student portfolio in which they provide tangible evidence of their ability to meet the course outcomes. At the end of the course, the Foundations Workshop marks will provide evidence of how a student has performed in each outcome area, for teachers, students and parents.

Component 3: The Projects

The Alberta provincial English curriculum is based on a model in which students are expected to demonstrate learning through performance. These projects are designed to allow the students to perform in a way that also shows their progress in each general outcome area. Our courses feature three projects: Minor Project #1, Minor Project #2 and The Major Project. Each of these has specific parameters placed on it, but we place a premium on student choice. As with the Windows, the Projects are meant to be culminations of student learning rather than course coverage. As such, they are not limited to a specific piece of literature or a unit of study, but rather student progress over a period of time.

"Projects are meant to be culminations of student learning rather than course coverage."

All students should be able to work within our parameters to find a learning task that is meaningful to them. The structure of each project reflects the learning outcomes that our students will be asked to display. For our full year students, for example, Minor Project #1 is devoted to General Outcome Areas One, Two and Five, Minor Project #2 is devoted to General Outcome Areas Three, Four and Five, and the Major Project encompasses all of the outcome areas (see Figure 1 for GLOs).

Minor Project #2 involves students in writing for a magazine that we created for a young adult demographic of 16-30 year olds, who "get fired up about things." The articles should represent the incredible diversity and passion that characterizes this generation. Figure 4 describes the submission criteria that the students must meet.

The Projects should work hand in hand with the Foundations Workshop as a way of allowing students, teachers and parents to see student progress in each of the outcome areas.

Reflection

Since we began our careers, we, like most of our colleagues, have been constantly working on improving our craft. Assignments get revised. Assessment systems get reworked. All of this is part and parcel of our professional duties. This year however, we tried something different: we let the kids in on the process. One of the first Windows assignments we asked our students to complete was to actually design a lesson based around our classroom reading of Henry Kriesel's short story, *The Broken Globe.* The story revolves around a fractured father/son relationship with the major issue being the father's medieval world-view and the son's passion for science. It's a rich story and we gave the students license to create any kind of lesson they wished, as long as they could ground the lesson in the curricular outcomes. We used this as a way of immersing the students in the curricular outcomes, while also introducing them to the basic tenets of backward design.

"But what do you want?"

This was very early on in the course and it was interesting to note how fundamentally limiting many of these student-created lessons were. To a large extent they spoke to a rather one-dimensional experience of the English language Arts – one dominated by worksheets and simplistic stimulus-response style questions. This assignment, in itself, went a long way towards establishing the need for what we were doing.

Throughout the course of the year, in virtually every assignment ranging from minor discussion-based in-class work to extensive written work completed primarily outside of class time, we have emphasized three aspects of our course structure:

1) The power of student choice
2) The importance of recognizing how the things we do connect with the course outcomes
3) That what we do in English class can matter beyond the classroom walls

In emphasizing these three aspects we have brought the basic tenets of learning, discovery and pedagogy to our daily classroom experience.

In every assignment we gave our students some degree of choice. For example, Minor Project #1 allowed students to choose form and structure to demonstrate mastery of the specific course outcomes, designated by us. There were also times where the degree of choice needed to be tempered, such as, choosing two out of a possible three works of literature around which to develop a topic. Initially, many students approached these choices with considerable trepidation, having likely had a very limited experience of choice in their previous English classes. In the early weeks of the class it was not uncommon to have a student ask – sometimes politely and sometimes with barely restrained exasperation – "But what do *you* want?" As the year progressed and students became more attuned to their own passions and process of development, that question stopped coming up – students began asking, "What do I want?" This shift from "you" to "I" represents a major paradigm shift. When a student asks us what we want they are really asking "What do I have to do to get a good mark?" This is a fair question to ask, given the pressure-packed, marks-driven society that we live in, but it is also a potentially debilitating question in that it reduces the English classroom to little more than a circus stage. These students might as well have been asking, "Which hoop do you want me to jump through?" In this process we move away from being the lion tamer; we put down our metaphorical whips and become the spotter in our students' trapeze stunt, there to stabilize the rope as opposed to carrying them over it.

Once students made the jump from "you" to "I" they began to take ownership of their own learning process and started to ask this question: "What do I need to do to be able to demonstrate that I can achieve this course outcome?" Students began to become aware not only of *what* they were doing, but *why* they were doing it. In her reflective letter at the beginning of her final Foundations Portfolio, one of our students wrote eloquently about this paradigm shift:

> I noticed this was the only English class I have ever taken where I was aware of the skills I was learning . . . Anyway, what I remember most about [her previous English class], was that whenever [her previous English teacher] gave us an assignment, she would tell us what to include and what not to include. She always gave us our assignments, and we never had anything called a minor or major project where we were given almost no restrictions, where we had to use our imaginations.

Another student wrote the following:

> The thing that separates this class from others is that there really isn't any "read this and answer these 50 questions" type of assignments where you wonder what your (sic) accomplishing besides

keeping yourself from failing. After reflecting back on my work it's really clear that each and every assignment has its own piece in puzzle, or brick in a foundation. The foundation we create in English 20-1 gives us something to build on for English 30-1. I can go further with this metaphor and say that the purpose every year preceding this one was to build a foundation for the next year until ultimately we graduate and decide what we want to do next.

Now, admittedly, we have been engaged in a process – the complete restructuring of our assessment system – that is far from the norm in every classroom, but we are convinced that the basic building blocks of this process are present in every classroom. While we may not all be revising our entire assessment system, certainly most of us are consistently tweaking that system. If we are not creating completely new assignments each and every day, we are surely making adjustments that will serve our students and our profession better in the long and short term. It is important to remember that we are not talking about a complete change in classroom practice, but instead we have established a pedagogical framework that should celebrate the great things that happen in classrooms everyday. Throughout this year we asked our students to approach everything with an open, but critical, mind. We wanted them to tell us when something simply did not work, and they did. They were engaged and invested in the success of this course and they were actively working to make it better. This is a process that every teacher could engage in, ranging from minor assignments to major elements of course design.

"By letting our students into our own teaching lives, we teach them how to ask real questions and demand real answers."

Throughout the course of the year, we – our students and ourselves – would recognize flaws in our methodology that sent us back – literally, in some cases – to the drawing board. Have we designed the perfect assessment system? Absolutely not, but it is a system that gets better with every set of revisions and with every bit of input our students bring to us. The very process of involving our students in establishing a framework for meaningful change has been a tremendous learning opportunity for them. It has taken some humility on our part and some faith on our students' part, as we discarded the mask of assessment expertise that so many of us wear to cover our own uncertainty and insecurity. By doing so, however, we have opened up a wider range of teaching and learning experience in our classroom.

Consider the following passage from Grant Wiggins' seminal text *Assessing Student Performance: Exploring the Purpose and Limits* of *Testing,* in which the author explores the etymology of the word assess:

> Assess is a form of the Latin verb assidere, to "sit with." In an assessment, one "sits with" the learner. It is something we do with and for the student, not something we do to the student. The person who "sits with you" is someone who "assigns value"

- the "assessor" (hence the earliest and still current meaning of the word, which relates to tax assessors). But interestingly enough, there is an intriguing alternative meaning to that word, as we discover in The Oxford English Dictionary: this person who "sits beside" is one who "shares another's rank and dignity" and who is "skilled to advise on technical points" (p. 14).

By inviting our students into the building process of the assessment relationship, we are not only building a more egalitarian base for the student-teacher relationship, but introducing our students to the concept of free, yet focused, inquiry that is at the heart of all genuine research. By letting our students into our own teaching lives, we teach them how to ask real questions and demand real answers. If we present our classrooms as living and growing entities that are shaped by constant reflection, we inspire our students to view their lives, both in and out of the classroom, in the same way. We talk to our students about metacognition as a means of further exploring the way that reflection can shape our practice. We show them that reflection has real-world applications, which has far-ranging implications for the English classroom.

If we ask our students to come with us on a journey to discovering a better assignment or a better classroom, it is not such a stretch to ask them to explore a work of literature with a sense of genuine possibility, rather than – as is too often the case – resigned expectation.

We can teach by modeling and kindling in our students an authentic sense of discovery that will serve them equally well in their study of literature and other disciplines as it will in their study of life. Ultimately, it is up to us to be thoughtfully fearless in our professional practice. If we are not prepared to ask ourselves the most difficult questions about our own practice – and do so with full transparency – we cannot claim to be meaningful guides to our students as they set about developing their own practice as scholars.

The introduction to one of our student's final Foundations Portfolio reflects our success. She eloquently articulates the connection between the power of the process, the learning that results and the long term possibilities.

> *The following portfolio is a representation of the long hard stressful struggle that this course has been. So after all of this: what have I learned? I think that I have gained a lot in taking this class. In previous years, I was given very specific outlines on what would and would not be accepted in an English course: use this format to write about this and this, and use these examples to support your thesis or else...suspense music. I found that I would do well in these*

classes only when I followed these instructions and noticed that if I were to stray from this formula, I was penalized. Other teachers forced me to write like a square, not allowing me to express what I thought about certain pieces of literature. However, <u>this</u> course has been like a breath of fresh air for me. You not only encouraged, but demanded, that I think outside of the box, instead of focusing on structure or what you thought were important details, I was allowed to communicate the feelings that I had towards the text; how I had connected with it. This course has ultimately broadened my horizons and has taught me that there is no one way to look at a piece of literature.

Let us end where we began with Virginia Woolf's *How Should One Read a Book:*

> *"The only advice, indeed that one person can give another about reading is to take no advice, to follow your own instincts, to use your own reason, to come to your own conclusions."*

When we read our students, we inherit a responsibility to read them well. We have a professional obligation to use our learning and professional judgment to speak to our students' needs and desires. As is the case with literary texts, students are equally as diverse from desk to desk, row to row, class to class and year to year. Our original goal was to develop an assessment framework that spoke to the diversity in needs and desires of each student. As a result of our work, we have discovered that the specific steps and outcomes of our process are not as important as the process itself. We are not asking teachers to necessarily adopt our structures, but rather to recognize the power of the process and to engage with their students to discover an assessment system that remains true to the ideals at the heart of all teaching and education. It is our fervent hope that the passion we have for learning, language and literature will inspire our colleagues and our students to find their way to an assessment system that speaks to students both in and beyond the classroom and will remain with them throughout their lives.

References

Wiggins, G. (1993). *Assessing Student Performance: Exploring the Purpose and Limits of Testing.* San Francisco, CA: Jossey-Bass.

Woolf, Virginia. (2002). How Should One Read a Book? In K. Evans, J. Hannaford, S. Poyntz et al (Eds), *Imprints* 12 Volume 2 (pp. 17-26). Toronto, ON: Gage Learning Corporation.

Melissa J. Noack

Melissa J. Noack, B.F.A., is currently an Art Teacher and Learning Area Leader for Visual and Performing Arts at Yarmouth High School in Yarmouth, Maine. She has been teaching Art for the past ten years and is working toward her Master's Degree in Education. Melissa has presented at national and state conferences on a variety of educational topics. She was a recipient of the Sallie Mae First Year Teacher Award, National Semi-Conductor Internet Innovator Award and most recently, the Milken Educator Award. Melissa enjoys networking with other educators from around the country to continuously improve her teaching and student learning.

Action Research and the Power of Peer Feedback

by Melissa J. Noack

As a High School Visual Arts teacher, I am a learner. One of the most galvanizing aspects of my profession is that I am encouraged to learn – daily, weekly, forever. This learning is acquired from a variety of sources: research, ongoing course work, professional development, and especially my students. It is inherently important for me to continue to improve my own teaching and learning so that my students will have the best possible educational experience. Ultimately, my goal as a teacher is to motivate students intrinsically: to engage them deeply in the process of learning so they desire and thirst to learn. The work described in this chapter only begins to scrape the tip of the iceberg.

Foundations for Success

Throughout the 2003-04 and 2004-05 school years, the students and I built a partnership in the learning process. They knew from the beginning that, together, we were piloting a new process for critiquing artwork called *Peer Feedback*. The students knew they were integral players in the process and were the key to its success. The students also understood from the beginning, that this was a "work-in-progress" and through their thoughtful feedback and debriefings, we would continue to improve this process until it was successful for the group as a whole.

It is essential, at the beginning of the year, to set the tone for the classroom and to make sure the expectations for students are clear. The environment in my classroom is one which encourages students to be safe, respected, and appreciated. It is also a culture that encourages risk-taking, especially in regards to creative problem-solving.

It should be noted that I always teach heterogeneously grouped students – students with mixed abilities, experiences, and grade levels. The *Action Research* process described here took place in an introductory Art course, called Foundations in Art. It involved two classes of 20 students each year. Some students entered the classroom with a strong artistic ability and lots of experience, while others may not have drawn anything since eighth grade. All students, however, are expected to show improvement throughout the year and especially from the midpoint critique to the final work of art. As a result of Peer Feedback, all students experienced growth and improvement over time (see Figures 6 to 10). The classroom culture was vital to the success of the process.

"The motivation for students developed from within; they wanted to present their best work to each other visually and orally."

The Action Research Process

In the developmental stages of this process, I stressed the importance of students relying on each other for feedback to improve their work; I never talked about how or if I was grading the peer feedback sessions. Students were focused on the concept of developing and refining their work. The motivation for students developed from within; they wanted to present their best work to each other visually and orally. They did this through rich, meaningful dialogues guided by the use of a protocol, (see Figure 1) while using Arts knowledge and vocabulary.

Figure 1

Student Interview Protocol
Metamorphosis Critique

Purpose:

To engage all students in giving and receiving feedback; To hear all students' voices through small group work.

Steps:

1. All students will fill out a written assessment before beginning the critique.

2. Teacher will identify 4 students who will interview 3 students. Teacher chooses the groups.

3. Teacher will review the purpose of the unit and review the protocol.

4. The four student interviewers begin, in small groups, and interview and record the answers to the three questions (see interviewers' questions below).

5. Upon completing the interviews, the interviewers gather in the middle of the room (fishbowl style) and report their answers to the rest of the class.

6. The interviewees listen carefully to the answers of each question and record common themes to each question.

7. The process is then debriefed, informally, as a large group.

Interviewers Questions:

While listening to the answers to the questions, what are the common themes you heard in response to the questions:

1. In what ways did the midpoint critique/feedback help you to produce high quality work?

2. If you did this project again, what would you add, change, or do differently?

3. List three important things that you learned about color from this unit or from working with guest artist.

Adapted from Fishbowl Seminar, *Protocols for Professional Learning Conversations*, by Catherine Glaude, with permission.

See page 121 for Blackline Master

The focus for the first year was to develop various strategies and formats for grouping students, and to engage all students in prolific, eloquent dialogues. In addition, I was practicing various learning strategies that I had acquired through taking a Differentiated Learning course. For example, I paid close attention to and recorded observations about where students were, according to their experience and readiness level. I grouped students by mixing readiness levels, so that they would receive a variety of perspectives on their work.

One of the standards in the Maine State Learning Results is to teach students how to discuss, analyze, and interpret their own work and the work of others, in order to develop a critical and informed artistic eye. In previous years, student critiques had not been successful, so using that data, I looked for a better way to achieve this goal.

The Action Research question that I started with was: *'How does Peer Feedback help to improve student work?'* I began the process by organizing students into small groups to critique each other's artwork. They became much more engaged in the class through dialoguing about their work, and they enjoyed the meaningful conversations using Arts knowledge and vocabulary. I knew this was a good beginning, but I wanted to take this concept to the next level where students would be held accountable for the feedback that they gave or received.

The following quotes are students' thoughtful perspectives regarding their own learning as a result of participating in Peer Feedback sessions:

> *"Critiques gave me an idea what I needed to improve and how I could approach my next project differently." ...B.O.C.*

> *"I think that the critiques helped me grow as an artist because I was able to learn from my mistakes in the midpoints and how to improve to finish the final piece and make it perfect." ...A.S.*

> *"Critiques were the most meaningful/beneficial to my overall personal growth. By getting another person's perspective, I could change my pieces and learn from my mistakes". ...S.G.*

> *"Critiques gave me insight on others thoughts compared to my own. After critiques I could change the troubled areas." ...R.A.*

> *"The critiques helped a lot in a way that I gained different techniques from others and I got different opinions from others about my work. I feel that I am a better drawer because of it!" ...J.C.*

> *"I found the critiques the most helpful because I'd never really had them before. Usually I'm the only one who sees my work and this was a pleasant change. It really helped me to look at my art from an objective point of view and learn how to improve." ...A.S.*

The Power of Peer Feedback

In the second year, the work moved to a different level. In addition to being engaged in rich dialogues about each other's work, students were asked to show evidence of Peer Feedback in their own work. They were to record the feedback from their peers and to demonstrate and explain how it helped them to improve their work and learning. The results, data, and evidence that I collected surrounding this process over two years were phenomenal; it was unbelievably energizing to see the increase in student achievement across the board on so many levels. The student work and testimonials provided clear evidence that this process was successful. For the most part, students have the desire to do their best work when they are motivated by their peers. With this process, the students are less dependent on me and are using each other for feedback and as valuable resources.

The following year, I continued this process but focused specifically on the feedback. Furthermore, I wanted students to document, use, and incorporate the feedback that they received during the midpoint critique; the students' work would be the evidence. The expectation was that through the participation in Peer Feedback sessions, the quality and creativity of the final product would increase, as well as the students' knowledge of essential learning.

I soon learned the process worked exceptionally well for a number of reasons. Students were relying on each other to give sound and meaningful feedback, which they documented during the midpoint critique and referred back to during their final critique. At that point, the students explained how they had used the feedback, referring to their work as evidence. They also discussed whether the feedback had made a difference in their final product, whether or not it was useful, and if so, how it had made a positive impact on their learning and understanding of the concepts.

Student-Directed Protocols

Another important aspect that contributed to the success of this process was the use of student-directed protocols. Having established a safe and open classroom culture where the climate and expectations were understood, it was a much easier task teaching students how to give and receive constructive criticism about their work. Because students knew and were very familiar with the criteria of the assignment, and because they had self-assessed their learning through the use of rubrics and answering reflective questions about their work, they could succeed at following a protocol and having rich, meaningful conversations.

Figures 2 and 3 are examples of protocols that I used and refined based on feedback from students during the first year. It shows my improvement in revising the first protocol to help students feel more successful. When they first began to use protocols, students indicated their need for more structure and support. In particular, their suggestion was to include prompts and ideas for what to say. This was a fabulous addition that greatly improved this tool. During the following school year, I continued to develop and revise the protocols, creating a variety of them. Figures 4 and 5 are examples of later protocols.

Students have been an integral part of the development of the different protocols. I ask them to give me feedback by discussing whether the process was helpful and meaningful for them and if not, what change could make it more effective. I collected their data in many ways: through written self-assessments and reflections, debriefing as a group and individually, and through my observations of the small groups. Students know that I truly value their feedback; they can see their results in the next protocol that they use.

Currently, I continue the process of developing strong and meaningful protocols for students; the purpose is to support them in making better quality and creative work, while increasing student understanding of the *essential knowledge*. (This refers to the overarching skills/concepts identified by each content area, based on the state's standards, by which students are graded.)

Figure 2 ▼

Foundations in Art
Requesting Feedback Protocol

The purpose of a protocol is to develop ground rules for your group to help focus or guide your discussion. It also evens the "playing field" among the members of your group; you will all have a chance to share and discuss your ideas.

The purpose of this Protocol is to **request feedback** on a specific technique or skill.

ALL STUDENTS MUST PREPARE AHEAD OF TIME. ALL STUDENTS WILL PRESENT. Decide in what area you would like feedback. This may be an area in which you have struggled or an area you may need to improve. This helps to focus the groups' attention and feedback.

Getting Started. Choose someone in your group to be a timekeeper and to keep the group on task.

Present to Group. The "Presenter" describes what he/she set out to accomplish. Explain the criteria of the assignment. Describe what particular part of the assignment was challenging or difficult for you. (This challenge area will direct your groups' feedback). All group members must remain silent during this presentation.

Questions. Group members ask clarifying questions about the presentation.

Reflection Time. All members of the group organize their feedback. Write notes as necessary.

Feedback. The group members brainstorm ideas and offer feedback RELATED to the challenge area. *It is important to offer constructive criticism.* The presenter remains quiet. He/she listens for any "nuggets" of information that may be helpful.

Conversation. The presenter invites the participants into a conversation to explore any of the feedback or ideas offered.

Debrief. Do a whip. How did this protocol work? How might we improve this for the future? Choose one member of your group to record this feedback and pass it in.

Adapted from Focused Feedback, Protocols for Professional Learning Conversations, by Catherine Glaude, with permission.

See page 122 for Blackline Master

Figure 3 ▼

Foundations in Art
Receiving Feedback Protocol

The purpose of this Protocol is to **offer constructive criticism to peers,** in regards to meeting the criteria of the assignment.

Please fill out the self-assessment ahead of time and review the rubric.

Step 1: (1 min) **Getting Started.** Choose someone in your group to be a timekeeper and to keep the group on task.

Step 2: (2 min) **Criteria of the Assignment.** The teacher will review the purpose and criteria of the assignment to the whole class.

Step 3: (5 min) **Present to Group.** The "Presenter" explains how the criteria of the assignment was met, in regards to creative problem solving skills and technical skills, referring to the rubric. All group members must remain silent during this presentation. Group members may take notes or formulate questions during the presentation.

Step 4: (5 min) **Feedback/Discussion.** The group begins the discussion, by asking questions to the presenter. One by one, each student asks a question to the presenter. The following is a list of questions to prompt your discussion. This will engage group members in a discussion. Please make sure everyone has time to ask at least one question.

Were you successful in communicating the idea creating a 3-dimensional space? Is your perspective convincing?
What strategies did you use to capture a 3-d space on a 2-d surface?
What makes your composition strong and interesting? Did you use the space well?
How well do your choice of colors work? Can you tell the difference between forms by the use of different values? Explain...
What mood is expressed by your color scheme?
Where do you fall on the rubric for creative problem-solving skills? technical skills?
Did you enjoy this assignment? Why or why not?
Do you feel you were successful in meeting the criteria of the assignment? Why or why not?
What were your challenges or difficulties with this assignment? How did you deal with these problems? What did you learn from this?
What would you do differently next time?
How will this assignment help your future assignments?

After all students have presented, write a short debrief in the space below. Choose a person to record the following:

Step 5: (3 min) **Learnings.** Do a whip. Everyone in the group has the opportunity to speak by saying what he/she learned from this practice OR what he/she is thinking of pursuing OR questions that were raised for him/her.

Step 6: (5 min) **Debrief.** We have modified this protocol throughout the year. Do you now feel comfortable with this process of talking about your work and giving and receiving feedback? Is there anything else we could add or change? As a group (please include a comment from each person), write short paragraph and pass it in.

Adapted from Focused Feedback, Protocols for Professional Learning Conversations, by Catherine Glaude, with permission.

See page 123 for Blackline Master

Figure 4

Midpoint Critique Feedback
Realistic Self-Portraits

Student Observation Protocol Purpose:
To give and receive feedback about the progress of your self portrait, before using charcoal.

1. Teacher will organize students in groups according to readiness.

2. Students will decide in what order they will present and who will be the facilitator.

3. The presenting student holds up their midpoint drawing next to his/her face. The group members are silent and stare at the sketch and the person for a solid minute.

4. Each group member records areas that need improvement as well as noting what the artist has done well.

5. One by one, each group member shares their feedback with the presenting artist. The presenting artist remains quiet and records the feedback.

6. After each group member has shared his/her feedback, the presenting artist asks for any clarifying questions or prompts questions to the group for additional feedback.

7. The above steps are repeated until each group member has presented.

8. The process will be debriefed orally, after all students have presented.

9. The teacher will photograph each student's sketch.

10. The teacher will print each student's sketch. The photograph of the sketch and the written feedback will be kept in each student's portfolio; both will become part of the final portfolio for the unit.

Adapted from Focused Feedback, *Protocols for Professional Learning Conversations*, by Catherine Glaude, with permission.

Figure 5

Foundations in Art - Drawing Unit
Final Critique Protocol

Purpose: To share your learning, techniques and skills with other students; To expand the interpretation of your work by encouraging different viewpoints and voices of others.

ALL STUDENTS WILL PRESENT.
Students will fill out the self-assessment ahead of time. Teacher will group students into clusters of 3 or 4 students per table.

1. (2 min) **Criteria of the Assignment.** The teacher will review the protocol, the purpose, and criteria of the assignment to the whole class.

2. (1 min) **Getting Started.** Choose someone in your group to be a timekeeper and to keep the group on task. Decide in what order each member will present.

3. (5 min) **Present to Group.** The "Presenter" describes how the feedback from the midpoint critique affected his/her final drawing. The presenter should show evidence by referring to the drawing. In addition, the presenter describes a piece of learning, technique or skill that was meaningful and significant (this may be a successful aspect of the drawing; you may also refer to your portfolio of progress). All group members must remain silent during this presentation.
Listening. As the presenter is speaking, each member of the group listens for and records one piece of evidence that shows the presenter understands and/or can demonstrate the essential learning of the assignment; or how the presenter has shown growth since the beginning of the year.

4. (2 min) **Feedback.** Each member, one by one, reads aloud, the documentation of evidence of learning or progress from his/her note card.

5. (2 min) **Final Word.** All group members hand their feedback to the presenter. The presenter reviews the feedback silently and chooses one that significantly stands out. The presenter reads it aloud to the group.

6. **Repeat steps 3, 4, and 5** until all members of the group have presented.

After all students have presented, write a short debrief in the space below. The facilitator records the following on a piece of paper to give the teacher. Include all names of group members.

7. (3 min) **Learnings.** What did you learn as a result of this unit of study? The facilitator records each group member's thoughts.

8. (3 min) **Debrief the process.** What worked well for you? What could we do differently next time to improve this process?

Adapted from Learning from Success Stories, *Protocols for Professional Learning Conversations*, by Catherine Glaude, with permission.

See page 124 for Blackline Master

Student work is evidence that this strategy is working. All students, even with differing experiences and ability levels, have achieved success by the end of each unit (see Figures 6 and 7). Through using sound protocols and engaging in rich, meaningful dialogues during midpoint critiques, students are able to reach this goal. Moreover, by encouraging students to rely on each other for feedback, they are becoming more self-directed and better problem-solvers. I have witnessed evidence of this through observing students and their work in the classroom. As the teacher, I am no longer the first person a student asks for feedback. Students are working towards finding solutions to creative problems collaboratively, in pairs, or in small groups.

The evidence supported my theory and improved the quality and creativity of the students' work. However, there are always challenges that occur with successes. The two biggest challenges that I encountered are dealing with group dynamics, and making sure the feedback that the students are receiving is accurate, helpful, and meaningful. I recently had a couple of students who felt that the feedback they received during the midpoint critique was not at all helpful. They thought the group members were just being agreeable and did not offer any specific ways to improve the work. The way I handled that was to recommend to those few students to be sure to see me for specific feedback after the midpoint critique if they did not get the feedback they felt was necessary. I continue to work on this aspect, as it is critical that all, not just select, students benefit from the Peer Feedback sessions.

Figure 6 ▼

Figure 7 ▼

Student engagement and motivation has increased tremendously in my classroom. Because students understand that their work will be viewed and constructively critiqued by their peers, not just by me, they are more motivated to do quality work. Because students are engaged and care about learning how to improve their work, I have experienced fewer classroom management and behavior problems; they practically ceased to exist. The entire process helps to create a collaborative learning environment which benefits all students, and thus, gives them a powerful learning experience! The progress and results of a sampling of student work are shown in Figures 8, 9, and 10.

"All students, even with differing experiences and ability levels, have achieved success by the end of each unit."

Student Work – Progress Over Time (Midpoint and Final Still Drawing)

Figure 8 ▼

Figure 9 ▼

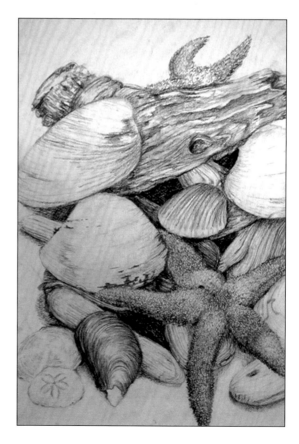

"Grades were never a motivational factor."

Conclusion

This has been an inspirational and highly beneficial process for both the students and for me. It is a process that engages students and encourages them to demonstrate higher level thinking skills without being formally evaluated or graded. Grades were never a motivational factor.

I learned that Peer Feedback sessions would not be quite so successful had they not been conducted through the use of protocols. With the students giving me feedback along the way, I developed many different protocols for them to use to structure their conversations. In addition to the use of protocols, the climate and culture in the classroom led to the huge success of this Action Research.

This type of research is a powerful and effective teaching tool, in that changes can be made immediately as the data are collected and reflected upon. This makes Action Research more meaningful and more likely to impact student learning.

Every year, the process continues to evolve and be refined. I now have documented evidence of success that I share with each new class; this becomes the building block for the current group of students. In conclusion, I will continue to revise, change, and reflect on my practice so that I am constantly improving my teaching and student learning. Collaborative work is a positive and galvanizing experience for everyone!

References

Coalition for Essential Schools. Box 1969, Brown University, Providence, RI, 02912. *www.essentialschools.org*

Davies, A. (2000) *Making Classroom Assessment Work.* Courtenay, BC: Connections Publishing.

Glaude, C. (2005). *Protocols for Professional Learning Conversations: Cultivating the Art and Discipline.* Courtenay, BC: Connections Publishing.

McDonald, J.P., Mohr, N., Dichter, A., and McDonald, E.C. (2003). *The Power of Protocols: An Educator's Guide to Better Practice.* New York, NY: Teachers College Press.

Sagor, R. (1992). *How to Conduct Collaborative Research.* Alexandria, VA: ASCD.

Tomlinson, C.A. (1999). *The Differentiated Classroom: Responding to the Needs of all Learners.* Alexandria, VA: ASCD.

Note: The protocols used with the students, examples of student work, and student testimonials can be viewed at:
http://hs.yarmouth.k12.me.us/Pages/YSD_YHSTeachers/YSD_YHSMENo/noack0506/ art0506/melhome.htm

Catherine A. Glaude

Catherine A. Glaude, Ph.D., is an experienced educator and author with a strong background in curriculum, instruction, and assessment. She has taught elementary, middle, and secondary students, consulted at a state level, and instructed university and district classes. Currently, she is Principal of the William H. Rowe School and Facilitator of School Improvement for Yarmouth School Department in Maine. Catherine spends her time supporting team, professional, and organization development by offering tools and resources, as educators work toward improving student learning. For more Protocols, refer to her book, *Protocols for Professional Learning Conversations: Cultivating the Art and Discipline,* from Connections Publishing (2005).

Let the Conversations Begin in the High School: Using Protocols to Promote Dialogues Focused on Student Results

by Catherine A. Glaude

The goal of a *learning conversation* is to improve student learning. Collectively, educators possess a wealth of knowledge, skills, and experiences that are invaluable resources to each other. When the focus is on improving student learning, educators need each other to consider and inspect their practices against current research and draw upon their deep – and very practical – professional experience. There is much to be learned from these collaborative conversations. Structured, ongoing learning dialogue can be the most powerful professional development an educator will experience.

Why Use a Protocol?

A Protocol is a process for guiding a professional learning conversation. The purpose of a Protocol is to build the skills and promote the culture necessary for ongoing collaborative learning.

A Protocol:

1. Keeps a group focused in order to generate a wealth of helpful conversation and feedback in a limited amount of time

2. Encourages all members of the group to offer their most thoughtful and useful feedback and/or insights on a specific topic

3. Helps less verbal participants offer their voices into the conversation

4. Promotes thoughtfulness by allowing personal reflecting time within a group conversation

5. Encourages lively dialogue featuring multiple perspectives

6. Requires any individuals presenting their personal work to remain silent so that the feedback and insights offered from their colleagues are not lost

7. Reminds individuals to make observations rather than offering opinions, when conversations are focused on current research

8. Provides a safe and supportive structure for all to inspect their practices and results of the learning

Building a professional learning community takes time. The more directed a learning conversation is to an individual's practice, the more threatening it may become. However, the threat is replaced with enthusiasm about improving student learning, when focused conversations become the norm and individuals become skillful in learning together. Protocols enable the dialogue.

"Structured, ongoing learning dialogue can be the most powerful professional development an educator will experience."

How do Protocols Work?

Using Protocols to promote dialogue around a common reading assignment is less threatening than conversations focused on personal practice and student work. If a school or group has little experience in using Protocols for focused learning conversations, text-based discussions are a good place to begin. Learning communities with advanced skills in working together use these Protocols to stimulate rich and focused discussions. Following are three examples of Protocols: focusing on learning from text, getting feedback about professional goals, and looking at student work.

Learning Conversations Focused on Text

Text-based Protocols are easy to create when the purpose of the discussion is clear. Text-based Protocols may be used during team or faculty meetings. Discussion groups should be no larger than six members so all can contribute their thoughts. Group members should sit in a circle facing each other without tables in front of them. Note taking should not occur. Though it may feel unnatural at first, the procedure of having no table and not taking notes promotes deep listening to what others are saying. This sets the tone for how a group learns together. Surfacing Significant Ideas (Figure 1) is an example of a Protocol used for text-based discussions.

Learning Conversations Focused on Professional Goals or Challenges

Educators set professional goals for improving their practice and improving the learning of their students. Protocols will support educators as they reflect upon and refine work toward their professional goals. Feedback from others helps individuals consider new options for improving their work toward professional challenges and goals. Protocols may involve storytelling based on successful practices or challenging teaching incidences. Much can be learned from the collective experiences of colleagues. The storytelling Protocols attempt to harvest this collective wisdom. The Protocol, Learning From Success Stories (see Figure 2), is an example of a Protocol to promote reflection on a challenge.

Learning Conversations Focused on Student Work

Looking at student work has long been an individual teacher's task – something often done in the evening and in isolation from colleagues. Yet, student work should be the centerpiece of collaborative discussions about improving teaching and learning.

Figure 1 ▼

A SAMPLE PROTOCOL: SURFACING SIGNIFICANT IDEAS[1]

(Based on page 8, Protocols for Professional Learning Conversations)

Purpose of the Protocol:
To promote conversation around the ideas of a text that have personal significance to the readers; to surface personal perspectives and responses to significant ideas and extend the thinking and connection-making of the group.

Prior to the Conversation:
Everyone reads the same text and highlights two passages that represent the most significant ideas. Everyone should be prepared to share these passages and say why they are personally significant to them. If the text is short, the group may choose to read the text during the meeting.

(2 minutes) **Introduction.** A facilitator and timekeeper are designated. The ground rules and goal of the Protocol are reviewed.

(1 minute) **Write the Quote or Passage.** Each person writes his/her short passages on a strip of chart paper and tapes these to the wall. There should be one passage on each strip of paper. (People should write large enough so all group members can read the writing. The page number of the text should be written beside the passage.)

(30–45 min.) **Present the Ideas.** One person begins by presenting one Significant Idea from the text, stating why it is significant and what implication it has for his or her work. Members of the group add to this idea after the presenter speaks. Each person has up to seven minutes to discuss this Significant Idea. This process is repeated until each person has presented a Significant Idea. If a Significant Idea is connected to another person's Significant Idea, the strips of chart paper should be moved close together. After everyone has discussed their idea and if time is available, the second set of Significant Ideas may be presented and discussed.

(3 minutes) **Personal Write.** Participants record their ideas, connections and reflections quietly.

(3 minutes) **Closure.** The group summarizes what they have learned together. (If there are other small groups discussing the same text these groups may report one insight to the larger group.)

(3 minutes) **Debrief the Process.** Group members comment briefly on how the Protocol supported their learning and how they might improve upon the Protocol.

[1] The times indicated are guidelines and may be modified.

See page 125 for Blackline Master

Figure 2 ▼

A SAMPLE PROTOCOL: LEARNING FROM SUCCESS STORIES

(from Protocols for Professional Learning Conversations, page 26)

Purpose of the Protocol:
To learn from the successes of colleagues who faced a particular challenge.

Prior to the Conversation:
The group members are given a focus for their inquiry. Examples of inquiry focus areas are: Recall a time when you successfully helped your students understand and own the expectations for high quality work. Think of a success story you have had with a student who was struggling in your class. Each group member considers the focus and prepares what he/she will share with the group. This is best done with groups of six people.

(2 minutes) **Getting Started.** Select a facilitator and a timekeeper. Review the purpose of the Protocol and ground rules for this process. The focus statement is written on the board or on chart paper.

(40 minutes) **Storytelling.** In Round Robin style moving around the circle, each person tells his/her story without interruption, for up to five minutes.

Question and Answer. After each person tells his/her story people may ask questions for two to three minutes. The timekeeper keeps the process moving.

(5 minutes) **Learnings Debriefed.** In Round Robin style, moving quickly around the circle, each person says one thing he/she learned from these stories. (If there is a larger group each small group may report one group learning.)

(Note: The times indicated are guidelines and may be modified.)

See page 126 for Blackline Master

Figure 3 ▼

> **A SAMPLE PROTOCOL: FOCUSED FEEDBACK**
> *(from page 37, Protocols for Professional Learning Conversations)*
>
> **Purpose of the Protocol:**
> To focus the feedback a presenting teacher desires from the group.
>
> **Prior to the Conversation:**
> The presenting teacher identifies a focus question for his/her feedback session. (i.e. Is this work a good indicator of the student's ability to write persuasively? Are the criteria for this project clear? Can you see evidence that students are using the rubric to shape and improve their work?) For confidentiality and to remove potential bias, student names are removed and student work is labeled Student A, Student B, and so on. Copies of the work are made for everyone in the group. (Note: The times indicated are guidelines and may be modified.)
>
> (2 minutes) **Getting Started.** Select a facilitator and a timekeeper. Review the purpose of the Protocol and ground rules for this process.
>
> (5 minutes) **Context.** The presenting teacher offers the purpose for the assessment and any background information such as a rubric and/or criteria for the work. The focus question is written on chart paper or board for all to see.
>
> (8 minutes) **Review.** The group members review the student work in regard to the focus question. (If student work is lengthy, the work and the focus question may be given ahead of time.)
>
> (10 minutes) **Group Discussion.** Using the focus question as their guide, group members generate their insights and observation by what they see in the work. The presenting teacher is quiet.
>
> (10 minutes) **Dialogue.** The presenting teacher joins the discussion and directs conversation to any intriguing ideas or points to pursue.
>
> (5 minutes) **Reflection on the Conversation.** The group discusses how they experienced this conference and what they learned.

See page 127 for Blackline Master

Student work can be the context of some of the most meaningful and powerful professional development opportunities. The Protocol, Focused Feedback, (Figure 3) is an example of a Protocol used for collaborative inquiry around student work.

The Importance of Ground Rules

One indispensable tool when using Protocols is a set of ground rules (Figure 4). Ground rules describe behaviors that are necessary in order to have productive learning conversations. Ground rules keep participants honest to the process and the goal of the Protocol. A school or team may adopt one set of ground rules to be used with any Protocol. Ground rules should be written as behaviors. They should challenge a group to do its best learning together. A ground rule is added when a behavior is getting in the way of learning. For example, if arriving to meetings at the designated time is a challenge, then a ground rule about starting the meeting on time might be added. As well, a ground rule may be removed when it no longer challenges the group. A Protocol should allow time to reflect on the ground rules and make changes as needed.

Figure 4 ▼

> **GROUND RULES FOR LEARNING CONVERSATIONS**
>
> 1. Bring your most challenging, troublesome work to the conversation.
>
> 2. Celebrate feedback that challenges you to grow.
>   (Praise is nice to hear, but does not help you improve.)
>
> 3. Listen deeply. Do not rehearse what you plan to say while others are speaking.
>
> 4. Help others feel comfortable when sharing their thoughts and challenges.
>
> 5. Be mindful of the Protocol and keep the conversation focused.
>
> 6. Share the air and invite silent members into the conversation.
>
> *(Ground Rules from page 61, ©2005, Protocols for Professional Learning Conversations.)*

It is best to have a limited number of ground rules More than six ground rules may be too many for a group to remember. It is important to begin each learning conversation by revisiting the ground rules. The suggested Protocols outlined in this chapter are merely a starting point. As groups and facilitators become more skillful with professional learning conversations, they will begin to create their own Protocols.

The following questions may guide the development or adaptation of Protocols:

What is the purpose for the Protocol?

What learning do we need to do – together?

How much time is available for the learning conversation?

Who will join the conversation?

Are there existing group behaviors for which ground rules may be useful?

Are there any Protocols that we might adapt?

How do we prepare participants for the Protocol?

Another important point to consider is that Protocols are powerful tools for work with high school students. For example, text-based Protocols may be used or adapted for discussions with students. The Protocols guide thoughtful classroom discussions by requiring that students identify key ideas and support their answers with evidence from the text. The Protocols help students make meaning of a text while modeling good comprehension skills. As well, the Protocols involving collegial feedback on individual work may be adapted and used when students bring their work for peer feedback. Peer critique is a powerful way to involve students in the assessment process.

"Peer critique is a powerful way to involve students in the assessment process."

A skillful educator may create or adapt Protocols to promote and navigate both collegial and classroom learning. Like good teaching, some Protocols work best with some groups, while others must be adapted to suit specific and emerging needs. Using a Protocol to foster conversation is both an art and a discipline.

Note: This article is excerpted from *Protocols for Professional Learning Conversations*, by Catherine A. Glaude, published in 2005 by Connections Publishing, Courtenay, BC.

Linda D. Friedrich, Ph.D., is a Senior Research Associate at the National Writing Project at the University of California, Berkeley. Her research interests include teacher research, teacher leadership, professional development, professional learning communities, and the diffusion of knowledge. Prior to joining the National Writing Project in 2002, Linda served as Director of Research at the Coalition of Essential Schools. She earned her Ph.D. in Administration and Policy Analysis at Stanford University's School of Education. Before becoming a researcher, Linda facilitated professional development and middle school reform at the Philadelphia Education Fund.

Linda Friedrich & Paul LeMahieu

Paul G. LeMahieu, Ph.D., has a career in educational research and evaluation, as well as policy and practice, that spans over thirty years. He has directed research organizations; taught research methods, psychometrics, and educational policy; and held executive and senior policy positions in state departments of education and local education agencies. Paul is currently the Director of Research, Evaluation and Information Systems for the National Writing Project at the University of California, Berkeley. He is also an affiliated faculty member in the College of Education at the University of Hawai'i - Mānoa. His scholarly interests focus on educational assessment and accountability, as well as classroom learning and the professional development and policy environments that support it.

Looking at Student Work to Build an Evaluative Framework: Why…and More Important, How?

Paul G. LeMahieu and Linda D. Friedrich

Everyone looks at student work. These days, everyone knows not to develop assessment systems without doing so. It has become a mantra, a sort of talisman that at best imparts rigor and quality and at the very least, lends an apparent credibility to any development effort. Unfortunately, there is too little guidance about why and how to do so – the kind of deep, thoughtful guidance that can not only provide procedural direction, but also ensure that the student work is "looked at" in constructive ways, in order to develop systems that enhance students' learning.

In this chapter, we want to describe a process for using and involving student work in the development of an assessment system. The inductive approach that we offer allows the elicitation of an evaluative framework from and out of student work; testing and refining it by reference to new work; and finally, validating it through application to yet more work. Perhaps as important, the inductive approach that we suggest also develops the school into a focused, professional community – one that is capable of using assessment to invite increased effort and improved performance of its students.

Our inductive approach to building an evaluative framework serves three broad purposes. The process we propose seeks to:

1) support the development of an evaluative assessment framework with the potential for constructive use

2) build common and widely held understandings of the meaning of the evaluative framework and its application

3) form a community of assessment use that employs such an evaluative framework wisely and well

This process has been used in diverse settings to accomplish a number of goals. In Pittsburgh, PA it was used to develop an assessment framework for a district-wide assessment of writing portfolios. The resulting framework had sufficient technical rigor to replace the standardized writing assessments then used for public accountability purposes (LeMahieu, Gitomer, and Eresh, 1995; LeMahieu, Eresh, and Wallace, 1992). In Arkansas, it has been used to develop assessment frameworks for use statewide across the four core content areas (English language arts, mathematics, science and social studies). In a number of schools in Hawai'i, the process guided a series of school/community events to explore a form of "lateral accountability" that provided a critically honest, yet fair assessment of school performance and its causes. These events engaged the community simultaneously in understanding and supporting school improvement efforts (LeMahieu, 1996).

"...testing practice now is, at best, confused and conflicted and at worst, an impediment to what many know to be best practices in teaching and learning."

The Reform of Assessment and the Place of Assessment in Reform

As researchers and measurement specialists, we are struck by a central irony of our endeavor: the world seemingly alternates between first paying no attention and then too much (and often the wrong kind of) attention to what we do. After decades of simply being ignored, testing practice now is, at best, confused and conflicted and at worst, an impediment to what many know to be best practices in teaching and learning. The reason for this often sorry state of affairs is a lack of thoughtful clarity about policy, programs, and practice in testing and assessment.

Many (especially policy makers) look to testing as an agent of change and reform. Implicitly, they assert an intuitively attractive, common sense argument about expectations, assessments, and attendant accountability incentives. It is suggested that the clear articulation of goals will make public the expectations for individuals and the system; appropriate and adequate assessment will reveal the performance of individuals, schools, and systems; and ties to appropriate sanctions and rewards will provide the motivation to improve effectiveness and productivity.

Large scale assessment systems are rarely as transparent about expectations as the public might assume. Further, externally administered tests, which are necessarily infrequent and not tied closely to the work in particular classrooms or schools, fail to provide regular, timely and relevant feedback upon which students and teachers can rely, to confront misconceptions about content and to nurture students' ongoing growth and development. Incentives in the form of test scores, grades, political and material consequences and the like, do not motivate students to deeply engage in a given subject matter or to take responsibility for their own learning. In fact, such incentives, in some cases appear to have unintended negative consequences, including the promotion of superficial learning.

Teachers take on these challenges as they work to build classroom and school assessments and to refine their own teaching in order to better promote students' learning and development. They are making public the expectations of performance and the hallmarks of quality (e.g., through the use of checklists and rubrics that highlight important content). Educators are also emphasizing the importance of creating assessments to go to the heart of a particular subject matter (e.g., the development of careful observational skills in the biological sciences) and to incorporate students' own learning goals.

"...expectations are the single greatest determiner of student performance over which we have direct and immediate control."

While we are not altogether optimistic about the impact of current testing and accountability mandates, this movement put forth by teachers illustrates exactly why we are optimistic about and committed to the place of assessment in educational reform. Individually and collectively, they demonstrate considerable courage in their efforts to develop and provide illustrations of assessment tasks and processes, as well as evaluative frameworks used to constructive effects in the classroom. For example, the chapters in this book amply demonstrate the power of clear public expectations tied to a rational view of instruction in which many decisions are made better by informing them with high quality and relevant evidence. Teachers know that the assessments that we use embody our institutional expectations for students, and that expectations are the single greatest determiner of student performance over which we have direct and immediate control.

Research also tells us that the expectations that students encounter in schools are not as high as they should be and they are not evenly applied. Expectations are not consistent from classroom to classroom and, sad to say, there are some for whom we have lower expectations than others. Working across the school to develop a shared set of high and consistent expectations for student performance is a challenge. We offer one approach that can be formalized and embedded within a school's norms and operating procedures to engender a true community of practice, guided and informed by constructive assessment. In the following pages, we describe a vision and procedures for developing and then embedding a system of assessment rooted in student work, within a school community.

Working Together to Build an Assessment Community

This approach to the development of an assessment framework draws upon teacher research traditions to build an inquiry community that matures over time, in terms of both its substantive sophistication and the inherent expectations employed in its assessments. The process begins with the identification of a design team who will engage in the development of the assessment framework. The team should be broadly representative of the range of programs within the subject area that is the focus of the assessment. In addition to participating in the development of the evaluative framework, the design team is also responsible for communications with the rest of the faculty, keeping them informed of and bringing them along with the team's work.

Each member of the design team selects three students to follow over time, one low, middle, and high performer, so that the framework that is induced out of the students' work will be broadly applicable. Similarly, adequate representation of all significant populations (e.g., sex, ethnicity, special needs, etc.) should be included among the collection of students studied.

This design team will meet several times over the course of a year or so. This permits an iterative process in which student work is examined, an evaluative framework elicited, and classroom practice reconsidered, as the emerging framework challenges teachers to expand their practice. At these meetings, members bring work from each of the three students they are following; the student work analyzed should reflect the full range of assignments and types of products to be evaluated through the framework (e.g., projects, students' metacognitive reflections on their learning, presentations). These conversations may also generate insights that result in the piloting and adoption of new classroom practices and activities.

The teams organize themselves by defining the roles of facilitator (who guides the assessment conversations), recorder (who documents the conversations), and discussants (who participate in the evaluative conversations). The individuals serving in these roles rotate so that every member of the development team does each job.

An Inductive Approach to the Development of Evaluative Frameworks

The inductive approach to developing an assessment framework grounded in student work proceeds through three phases: 1) *Exploration,* 2) *Confirmation,* and 3) *Validation.* The purpose and activities of each step are unique, and collectively they suggest a means of inspecting student work to ground the assessment development. While we present these phases as separate, distinct, and sequential, in practice each informs the others, and certain activities located in one may be revisited later as evidence and experience suggests.

Exploration

In this phase, an exploratory process is invoked to elicit a sense of what the community values, what it will look for in student work, and just how evidence of those qualities will appear in that work. The design group begins by closely examining one student's work. That examination is guided by the initiating question, "What does this work tell us about this student as a(n) writer (or scientist, or historian, or mathematician, or learner, as appropriate)?" After individually reading and recording reactions privately, the design group engages in what is typically a lively and rewarding professional conversation that seeks to answer its guiding question.

"...the point of education is to produce doers; learners who will (and are) using their knowledge."

We should say in passing that there are many possible constructions for this opening question. We like this one as it suggests that the point of education is to produce doers, learners who will (and are) using their knowledge. We can assure that the resulting conversation is a very professionally rewarding one. One teacher says "I see a writer with a sense of humor." Another, "I see one with great control of grammar, punctuation and the like." And a third, "I didn't notice those things, but I certainly see one who is struggling with writing dialog – perhaps that's something new for her."

As this conversation proceeds, the facilitator's job is to keep it moving and focused on the question at hand (in this case, "What does this work tell us about this student as a writer?"). There are a number of wonderful resources to help the facilitators with their work (see, for example: Allen and Blythe, 2004; MacDonald, et al., 2003; Weinbaum, et al., 2004; Glaude, 2005). Collectively, these resources suggest ways of addressing issues such as sensitivity to the vulnerabilities of public exposure of one's practice, the importance of norms of respect for colleagues and for students, and so on. The recorder documents the conversation, specifically to note those points of "evaluative judgment" being exercised (along with the evidence cited to support them). Thus, in documenting the points made by the teachers above, the recorder might list: "sense of humor," "control of grammar and punctuation," "trying new things."

Note that the recorder is not concerned with the judgment being made (i.e., whether the student's performances are thought to be good or bad) – just the basis for the judgment: the element being examined (the "point of evaluative judgment") and the evidence that is referenced in that examination.

Several minutes are spent on the first student's work before moving on to a next and a next. With each new student's work, the roles of facilitator and recorder rotate, so that everyone gets to participate in the discussions. By the time all of the student work has been discussed (especially across a number of meetings over the year) there is quite a lengthy list of "points of evaluative judgment" that has been enumerated.

Next it is time to analyze that list. There will be a number of similar elements – many can be combined. There will be conceptually related items – these can be grouped under common dimensions with the specific elements as illustrations. There will be redundant items as several of the teachers see and say the same things – these can be eliminated. Over time, redundant observations occurring across assignments and students may indicate that it is time to move into the next phase of the process.

Figure 1 ▼

Dimensions and Elements of Portfolio Scoring Rubric

1. Accomplishment in Writing
- Meeting worthwhile challenges
- Establishing and maintaining purpose
- Use of the techniques and choices of the genre
- Control of conventions, vocabulary and sentence structure
- Awareness of the needs of the audience (organization, development, use of detail)
- Use of language, sound, images, tone, voice
- Humor, metaphor, playfulness

2. Use of Processes and Strategies for Writing
- Effective use of prewriting strategies
- Use of drafts to discover and shape ideas
- Use of conferencing opportunities to refine writing (peers, adults, readers)
- Effective use of revision (reshaping, refocusing, refining)

3. Growth, Development and Engagement as a Writer
- Evidence of investment in writing tasks
- Increased engagement with writing
- Development of sense of self as a writer
- Evolution of personal criteria and standards for writing
- Ability to see the strengths and needs in one's writing
- Demonstration of risk-taking and innovation in interpreting writing tasks
- Use of writing for varied purposes, genres and audiences
- Progress from early to late pieces, growth, development

Figure 1 illustrates the result of one example of this sort of analysis and conceptual organization. In this case, the process was applied to develop a framework for evaluating student writing portfolios (Wolf, Bixby, and Gardner, 1991). Across several students and meetings, the design team created lists of points of evaluative judgment that literally "covered the walls." In turn, the team analyzed, synthesized, and reorganized these lists to produce the framework in Figure 1.

One notes a number of important points about the evaluative framework presented in this figure.

First, the elements included remained after eliminating redundancy and combining similar points of evaluative judgment, much as is suggested above. Entries such as "Use of language, sound, image, tone, voice" combine several similar "points of evaluative judgment" into a single (admittedly compound) element. Second, conceptual groupings organize these elements and form the overarching dimensions that structure the framework. These larger dimensions were used in making evaluative judgments, with the elements employed as illustrative exemplars. Third, the resulting framework permitted deep insight into writing. In fact, the teachers who participated in its development successfully used it to promote and guide discussions about student accomplishment – both among professionals and with students. These conversations genuinely contributed to students' increased efforts and improved performance. However, attaining such insights depended on their participation in a development process parallel to that described here. Having drawn the evaluative framework out of these examinations of student work, it is now time to begin to test that framework.

Confirmation

The exploratory phase above will produce an evaluative framework that is firmly rooted in the students' work which served as the focus of the assessment conversations. This is why it is critical to follow students who are broadly representative of those to whom the framework will be applied. Even given such a sampling, there is a risk that the resultant framework will describe the student work wonderfully, but unfortunately do so only for those types of students included in the development sample.

Consider, as an extreme case, the instance where all of the students' work examined at the exploratory stage happens to be from low achievers. The resulting framework might fit their work very well, but it would have a "ceiling effect," lacking sufficient "top" to capture the performance of highly accomplished writers. Not only would it fail to give such writers an opportunity to reveal the full measure of their accomplishment, it would also hold out expectations that are too low for *all* students.

This issue is addressed during the confirmatory stage by applying the emerging evaluative framework to a new set of students' work. At this stage the initiating question changes from a broad exploratory one, to one that applies the emerging framework. For example, the design group might now ask, "How would you judge this student's performance on each dimension of our framework? Upon what evidence would you base that judgment?"

It is useful to provide an open-ended worksheet organized around the framework. Something like the framework offered in Figure 1, with appropriate open space for recording clinical notes in subsequent examination of students' work, serves this purpose well. While examining the student work, each development group member makes notes capturing his or her judgments, relevant evidence, and their rationale. Then all team members share their views in an open conversation.

At this stage the recorders document the judgments and the evidence supporting those judgments. In analyzing the resultant data, particular attention is paid to:

1) any dimensions that are ambiguous or poorly understood by the development team

2) judgments made that are not reflected in the framework (for which the framework may need to be revised)

3) dimensions and elements of the evaluative framework that cannot find evidence in the work to support judgments

"…explicit use of reflection was introduced into their classes."

On occasion, the framework may check for some attribute(s) that the work does not reveal. At times, the student in question does not exhibit the attribute; at others, the assignment under consideration does not ask it of him/her. In some instances, the student may work in a classroom that doesn't value or address a particular attribute. In this last case, the development team may brainstorm the classroom practices that do engender the desired outcomes and commit to using them in their classes before the next team meeting (when relevant student work could then be examined).

A good example concerns the introduction of student reflection into the community of practice that developed the framework in Figure 1. While confirming the framework, the teacher/developers noted their desire to assess students' awareness of their own learning (e.g., their assessment of their own performance; their sense of what accomplished performance looks like; their awareness of their own learning needs and how to address them; and the like.) They were, however, disappointed by the lack of consistent evidence upon which to base such assessments. Therefore, they brainstormed the kind of classroom events that would provide relevant opportunities and with them, the evidence for assessment. The developers used and refined these strategies in their practice and thus, explicit use of reflection was introduced into their classes (Camp, 1990).

Through this iterative process – examining students' work and reflecting on the classrooms that produce it – a tremendous shaping of instruction and classroom practice can occur. The confirmatory process drives classroom change as well as subsequent revision of the framework.

Validation

At this point, the design group has developed a well-refined framework that anticipates a wide range of products. Those involved in its creation have deep understanding of the framework and have truly developed "wise eyes" for looking at student work. The design group must now ask whether it has developed something that only its members understand or something that is more generally useful. Is it possible to explain clearly and unambiguously to others the meanings of the framework and its several dimensions and elements? This happens by bringing others (including faculty, students or parents) into the conversation, as we move from use by the design team only to use by others in the school community.

At this stage, anchor work (exemplars that are held by consensus to illustrate each level of performance) is selected and evaluative commentary written in the form of clinical notes explaining why there is such strong agreement regarding what each illustrates. In addition, if there is an intent to aggregate and summarize results for external audiences, a quantitative scale can be added at the level of the dimensions. Then colleagues are brought in and trained in the use of the system, replicating in short form the development process used up to now. The levels of agreement in their assessments, and even the relationships between scores on the newly developed system and other measures of achievement, can be explored.

This development process will result in an evaluative framework that may be located on a conceptual continuum, from the very simple to the sublimely subtle and complex. At one end are assessments that can be very easily shared with others (such as, scoring of multiple choice examinations) but they tend to avoid complex performances and lack deep insight into student work. At the other end of the continuum are assessments that are very insightful indeed, but difficult to apply easily and with widespread agreement. The validation phase seeks to ensure that the evaluative framework in use is as welcoming of complex outcomes and assessment insights as possible, while still being generally useful. Validation also represents the first stages of a process of building a larger community that can become increasingly sophisticated in its judgments and better able to apply more subtle and insightful frameworks. In short, over time, professional communities can develop "wise eyes" for looking at student work.

Developing "Wise Eyes" Together:
The Impact on a Professional Community

In our experience, two things have invariably been realized through these "assessment conversations." First, all who participate in them leave with higher and more clearly articulated aspirations for student performance. The derivation of criteria and expectations for quality in student work is built upon by professionals adding to each other's list. These assessment conversations proceed until the final set of criteria is far greater than the initial one or that of any individual teacher.

Secondly, a shared interpretive framework for regarding student work emerges from these assessment conversations. Aspirations and expectations become commonly understood across professionals and more consistently applied across students. The long-term, collaborative design of these conversations supports this outcome.

"Where expectations are high and represent attainable yet demanding goals, students strive to respond and ultimately achieve."

While we have described a process that engages professionals in building an evaluative framework, we believe that this process can be adapted to engage students as well. Some teachers emphasize building students' ownership over their learning, as well as developing their understanding of what constitutes excellent performance. Imagine the potential contributions of a streamlined version of this process in building students' vision of and commitment to achievement. Further, the understanding of how the adults within their school community have worked to build shared and consistently applied expectations will appeal to young people's sense of fairness and equitable treatment.

These two outcomes of assessment conversations – elevated aspirations and more consistently held and applied expectations – are key ingredients in a recipe for beneficial educational change. The relationship between expectations and student performance is compellingly documented by research. Where expectations are high and represent attainable yet demanding goals, students strive to respond and ultimately achieve. Assessment conversations focused upon student work enable this. What remains is to engage the whole of the professional community in a commitment to participating in these conversations. Structuring them as we suggest ensures these beneficial impacts and provides a powerful investment in the human side of the educational system.

References

Allen, D. and Blythe, T. (2004). *The Facilitator's Book of Questions: Tools for Looking Together at Student and Teacher Work.* New York: Teachers College Press and Oxford, OH: National Staff Development Council.

Camp, R. (1990). Thinking together about portfolios. *The Quarterly* of *the National Writing Project and the Center for the Study of Writing,* Vol. 12 (2), pp. 8-14, 27.

Gitomer, D.H. (1993). Performance assessment and educational measurement. In R.E. Bennett and W. C. Ward (Eds.) *Construction versus choice in cognitive measurement* (pp. 241-263). Hillsdale, NJ: Lawrence Erlbaum.

Glaude, C. (2005). *Protocols for Professional Learning Conversations.* Courtenay, BC: Connections Publishing.

LeMahieu, P.G., Eresh, J.T. and Wallace, Jr., R.C. (1992). Using Student Portfolios for public accounting. *The School Administrator.* Journal of the American Association of School Administrators. Vol. 49, (11). Alexandria, VA.

LeMahieu, P.G., Gitomer, D. A. and Eresh, J.T. (1995). Portfolios in large-scale assessment: Difficult but not impossible. *Educational Measurement: Issues and Practice.* Journal of the National Council on Measurement in Education. Vol. 13 (3).

LeMahieu, P. G. (1996). From authentic assessment to authentic accountability. In Armstrong J. (Ed.) *Roadmap for change: A briefing for the Second Education Summit.* Education Commission of the States. Denver, CO.

McDonald, J. P. Mohr N., Dichter A., and. McDonald, E.C. (2003). *The Power of Protocols: An Educator's Guide to Better Practice.* New York: Teachers College Press.

Weinbaum, A., Allen, D., Blythe, T., Simon, K., Seidel, S. and Rubin, C. (2004). *Teaching as Inquiry: Asking Hard Questions to Improve Practice and Student Achievement.* New York: Teachers College Press and Oxford, OH: National Staff Development Council.

Wolf, D.P., Bixby, J., Glenn, J. and Gardner, H. (1991). To use their minds well: Investigating new forms of student assessment. In G. Grant (Ed.), *Review of Research in Education* (Vol. 17, pp. 31-74). Washington, DC: American Educational Research Association.

Wolf, D.P., LeMahieu, P.G. and Eresh, J. T. (1992). Good measure: Assessment in service to education. *Educational Leadership*, Vol. 49 (8), pp. 8-13.

Epilogue

Each author in this book writes from personal experience. Each has risked inviting students into the assessment *for* learning process without a 'net'. Each models with students and colleagues what it means to learn from missteps, to seek feedback, to keep a sense of humor and to apply insights from both failures and successes in order to strengthen their students' learning. Their individual and combined voices affirm the power of assessment *for* learning and make concrete the research findings from around the world. By offering an array of possibilities, they invite readers to join in and make a difference for learning in their own settings.

"If we are not prepared to ask ourselves the most difficult questions about our own practice – and do so with full transparency – we cannot claim to be meaningful guides to our students as they set about developing their own practice as scholars."
-- Brent McKeown and Scott Horton

The themes of Book One have focused on bringing students directly into the assessment *for* learning process by ensuring that they have a clear understanding of their learning destinations, are actively engaged with teachers in creating criteria that bring learning destinations into sharp focus, and are prepared to provide and make effective use of feedback to strengthen their work.

Book Two continues and builds on these themes by highlighting a variety of strategies that teacher-authors have used to structure and guide student collection and selection of evidence, which becomes proof of learning. Chapters in this book also invite readers to carry insights from assessment *for* learning into a careful reconsideration of what counts and what matters in marking and determining final grades. Broadening the range of formats and strengthening the ability of students to take a significant role in reporting their learning, within and beyond the classroom, are continuing threads in this book.

Appendix:

Blackline Masters

The following Blackline Masters are provided for teachers to adapt to their own use in schools. Please ensure the copyright information appears on every page that is copied.

To enlarge to 8 1/2 x 11 inches, set photocopier at 123% and align top edge of page with corresponding edge of copier glass.

Editor's Name _____   Writer's Name _____

Proofreading Exercise for Creative Writing

As peer editors, each of you will peruse (read carefully) at least two students' works and identify aspects of each according to the chart below. It is vital to provide constructive criticism, or warm and cool feedback. Don't simply say, "Nice job!" and draw a little smiley face. Become both teacher and critic, and through this you will improve your writing. You must use the constructive criticism of your peers to improve your piece; if you're unsure about it, see me.

WARM SIDE!!!

Place: Identify **two** showing details that take you to this place.

1. _____
2. _____

Character: Identify **two** showing details that help you experience who these characters are.

1. _____
2. _____

Dialogue: Identify **two** strong examples of real use of dialogue.

1. _____
2. _____

Action: Identify **two** showing details that help you to see or perceive the action.

1. _____
2. _____

Conflict: Identify the **major** conflict of this story.

_____
_____

Resolution: How is this conflict resolved?

_____
_____

Write two examples of strong, showing word choice.

1. _____
2. _____

Identify **two** well-crafted phrases or sentences that enhance the story.

1. _____
2. _____

COOL SIDE

Write **two** examples of weak, telling (not showing) word choice.

1. _____
2. _____

Place: Identify **two** telling (not showing) details that try to describe this place.

1. _____
2. _____

Character: Identify **two** telling (not showing) details about these characters.

1. _____
2. _____

Dialogue: Identify **two** weak examples of dialogue.

1. _____
2. _____

Action: Identify **two** telling (not showing) details about action.

1. _____
2. _____

Identify **two** weak phrases that are confusing and/or don't follow the story.

1. _____
2. _____

Check the column that applies to the category.

	Excellent	Good	Average	Poor
Showing details				
Organization (effective beginning and ending)				
Cohesion				
Voice				
Sense of character, action, and place				
Word choice				
Grammar				

Comment on any of those categories.

_____
_____

Also suggest ways of improving this piece...

_____
_____

From *Classroom Assessment: What's Working in High Schools?* A. Davies and K. Busick (Eds) © Connections Publishing. May be reproduced for classroom use.

After reviewing my writing, I feel I have these:

3 strengths:

_____

_____

_____

2 areas I want to improve:

_____

_____

Next time, I'll . . .

Writer: _____ Date: _____

After reviewing my writing, I feel I have these:

3 strengths:

_____

_____

_____

2 areas I want to improve:

_____

_____

Next time, I'll . . .

Writer: _____ Date: _____

After listening to you, I understood:

3 things:

_____

_____

_____

2 questions I have:

_____

_____

Next time, I'd like to add . . .

Writer: _____ Date: _____

After listening to you, I understood:

3 things:

_____

_____

_____

2 questions I have:

_____

_____

Next time, I'd like to add . . .

Writer: _____ Date: _____

Après avoir vu _____ en français:
(After having seen…)

J'ai compris (I understood) ces 3 choses (things) essentielles:

1.
2.
3.

J'ai entendu (heard) ces mots ou ces expressions:

_____   _____   _____
_____   _____   _____
_____   _____   _____
_____   _____   _____
_____   _____   _____
_____   _____   _____
_____   _____   _____
_____   _____   _____
_____   _____   _____

J'ai des questions ou Je n'ai pas compris:

_____
_____

Ma partie favorite était: (My favorite part was…)

Nom: _____   **Date:** _____

Home Performance by _____ Date: le _____

(Devoirs pour la classe de français)

I will tell the story, _____

Please notice:

_____

_____

_____

And watch for :

    Body Language   Acting   Speaking French   Eye Contact   Enthusiasm

Home Audience Response by _____

After listening to and watching your storytelling, I'd like to specifically compliment you on:

_____

_____

Home Performance by _____ Date: le _____

(Devoirs pour la classe de français)

I will tell the story, _____
Please notice:

_____

_____

_____

And watch for :

    Body Language   Acting   Speaking French   Eye Contact   Enthusiasm

Home Audience Response by _____

After listening to and watching your storytelling, I'd like to specifically compliment you on:

_____

_____

What topic(s) have we already learned that connect to the present topic?

Topic:

Connection:

Topic:

Connection:

Topic:

Connection:

What topic(s) have we already learned that connect to the present topic?

Topic:

Connection:

Topic:

Connection:

Topic:

Connection:

Criteria	In Progress	Finished Product
	Looks good: Work on:	
	Looks good: Work on:	
	Looks good: Work on:	
	Looks good: Work on:	

Figure 13 - Polly Wilson   **119**

Conference Preparation Questions

Please answer each question carefully using specifics so that your opinion will be well represented.

1. In general, how would you describe your progress?

2. Do you think that your grade is an accurate reflection of your knowledge in this class?

3. Is there any material that you find difficult to understand?

4. Can you suggest any way to make this material easier to understand?

5. Specifically, describe how your work meets the expectations in this class.

6. Describe your strengths in this class and at school in general.

7. Describe your level of involvement and your contributions when participating in group assignments.

8. What work have you completed that you are proud of?

9. Can you identify any actions (improve study habits, participation etc.) that will help you to be more successful in class?

10. What steps can your teacher or parents take to support you in becoming more successful?

Student Interview Protocol
Metamorphosis Critique

Purpose:

To engage all students in giving and receiving feedback; To hear all students' voices through small group work.

Steps:

1. All students will fill out a written assessment before beginning the critique.

2. Teacher will identify 4 students who will interview 3 students. Teacher chooses the groups.

3. Teacher will review the purpose of the unit and review the protocol.

4. The four student interviewers begin, in small groups, and interview and record the answers to the three questions (see interviewers' questions below).

5. Upon completing the interviews, the interviewers gather in the middle of the room (fishbowl style) and report their answers to the rest of the class.

6. The interviewees listen carefully to the answers of each question and record common themes to each question.

7. The process is then debriefed, informally, as a large group.

Interviewers Questions:

While listening to the answers to the questions, what are the common themes you heard in response to the questions:

1. In what ways did the midpoint critique/feedback help you to produce high quality work?

2. If you did this project again, what would you add, change, or do differently?

3. List three important things that you learned about color from this unit or from working with guest artist.

Adapted from Fishbowl Seminar, *Protocols for Professional Learning Conversations*, by Catherine Glaude, with permission.

Foundations in Art
Requesting Feedback Protocol

The purpose of a protocol is to develop ground rules for your group to help focus or guide your discussion. It also evens the "playing field" among the members of your group; you will all have a chance to share and discuss your ideas.

The purpose of this Protocol is to **request feedback** on a specific technique or skill.

ALL STUDENTS MUST PREPARE AHEAD OF TIME. ALL STUDENTS WILL PRESENT. Decide in what area you would like feedback. This may be an area in which you have struggled or an area you may need to improve. This helps to focus the groups' attention and feedback.

Getting Started. Choose someone in your group to be a timekeeper and to keep the group on task.

Present to Group. The "Presenter" describes what he/she set out to accomplish. Explain the criteria of the assignment. Describe what particular part of the assignment was challenging or difficult for you. (This challenge area will direct your groups' feedback). All group members must remain silent during this presentation.

Questions. Group members ask clarifying questions about the presentation.

Reflection Time. All members of the group organize their feedback. Write notes as necessary.

Feedback. The group members brainstorm ideas and offer feedback RELATED to the challenge area. *It is important to offer constructive criticism.* The presenter remains quiet. He/she listens for any "nuggets" of information that may be helpful.

Conversation. The presenter invites the participants into a conversation to explore any of the feedback or ideas offered.

Debrief. Do a whip. How did this protocol work? How might we improve this for the future? Choose one member of your group to record this feedback and pass it in.

Adapted from Focused Feedback, *Protocols for Professional Learning Conversations,* by Catherine Glaude, with permission.

Foundations in Art
Receiving Feedback Protocol

The purpose of this Protocol is to **offer constructive criticism to peers,** in regards to meeting the criteria of the assignment.

Please fill out the self-assessment ahead of time and review the rubric.

Step 1: (1 min) **Getting Started.** Choose someone in your group to be a timekeeper and to keep the group on task.

Step 2: (2 min) **Criteria of the Assignment.** The teacher will review the purpose and criteria of the assignment to the whole class.

Step 3: (5 min) **Present to Group**. The "Presenter" explains how the criteria of the assignment was met, in regards to creative problem solving skills and technical skills, referring to the rubric. All group members must remain silent during this presentation. Group members may take notes or formulate questions during the presentation.

Step 4: (5 min) **Feedback/Discussion.** The group begins the discussion, by asking questions to the presenter. One by one, each student asks a question to the presenter. The following is a list of questions to prompt your discussion. This will engage group members in a discussion. Please make sure everyone has time to ask at least one question.

> Were you successful in communicating the idea creating a 3-dimensional space? Is your perspective convincing?
> What strategies did you use to capture a 3-d space on a 2-d surface?
> What makes your composition strong and interesting? Did you use the space well?
> How well do your choice of colors work? Can you tell the difference between forms by the use of different values? Explain...
> What mood is expressed by your color scheme?
> Where do you fall on the rubric for creative problem-solving skills? technical skills?
> Did you enjoy this assignment? Why or why not?
> Do you feel you were successful in meeting the criteria of the assignment? Why or why not?
> What were your challenges or difficulties with this assignment? How did you deal with these problems? What did you learn from this?
> What would you do differently next time?
> How will this assignment help your future assignments?

After all students have presented, write a short debrief in the space below. Choose a person to record the following:

Step 5: (3 min) **Learnings.** Do a whip. Everyone in the group has the opportunity to speak by saying what he/she learned from this practice OR what he/she is thinking of pursuing OR questions that were raised for him/her.

Step 6: (5 min) **Debrief.** We have modified this protocol throughout the year. Do you now feel comfortable with this process of talking about your work and giving and receiving feedback? Is there anything else we could add or change? As a group (please include a comment from each person), write short paragraph and pass it in.

Adapted from Focused Feedback, *Protocols for Professional Learning Conversations,* by Catherine Glaude, with permission.

Foundations in Art - Drawing Unit
Final Critique Protocol

Purpose: To share your learning, techniques and skills with other students; To expand the interpretation of your work by encouraging different viewpoints and voices of others.

ALL STUDENTS WILL PRESENT.
Students will fill out the self-assessment ahead of time. Teacher will group students into clusters of 3 or 4 students per table.

1. (2 min) **Criteria of the Assignment.** The teacher will review the protocol, the purpose, and criteria of the assignment to the whole class.

2. (1 min) **Getting Started.** Choose someone in your group to be a timekeeper and to keep the group on task. Decide in what order each member will present.

3. (5 min) **Present to Group.** The "Presenter" describes how the feedback from the midpoint critique affected his/her final drawing. The presenter should show evidence by referring to the drawing. In addition, the presenter describes a piece of learning, technique or skill that was meaningful and significant (this may be a successful aspect of the drawing; you may also refer to your portfolio of progress). All group members must remain silent during this presentation.

   Listening. As the presenter is speaking, each member of the group listens for and records one piece of evidence that shows the presenter understands and/or can demonstrate the essential learning of the assignment; or how the presenter has shown growth since the beginning of the year.

4. (2 min) **Feedback.** Each member, one by one, reads aloud, the documentation of evidence of learning or progress from his/her note card.

5. (2 min) **Final Word.** All group members hand their feedback to the presenter. The presenter reviews the feedback silently and chooses one that significantly stands out. The presenter reads it aloud to the group.

6. **Repeat steps 3, 4, and 5** until all members of the group have presented.

After all students have presented, write a short debrief in the space below. The facilitator records the following on a piece of paper to give the teacher. Include all names of group members.

7. (3 min) **Learnings.** What did you learn as a result of this unit of study? The facilitator records each group member's thoughts.

8. (3 min) **Debrief the process.** What worked well for you? What could we do differently next time to improve this process?

Adapted from Learning from Success Stories, *Protocols for Professional Learning Conversations*, by Catherine Glaude, with permission.
From *Classroom Assessment: What's Working in High Schools?* A. Davies and K. Busick (Eds) © Connections Publishing. May be reproduced for classroom use.

A SAMPLE PROTOCOL: SURFACING SIGNIFICANT IDEAS[1]

(Based on page 8, Protocols for Professional Learning Conversations)

Purpose of the Protocol:
To promote conversation around the ideas of a text that have personal significance to the readers; to surface personal perspectives and responses to significant ideas and extend the thinking and connection-making of the group.

Prior to the Conversation:
Everyone reads the same text and highlights two passages that represent the most significant ideas. Everyone should be prepared to share these passages and say why they are personally significant to them. If the text is short, the group may choose to read the text during the meeting.

(2 minutes)   **Introduction.** A facilitator and timekeeper are designated. The ground rules and goal of the Protocol are reviewed.

(1 minute)   **Write the Quote or Passage.** Each person writes his/her short passages on a strip of chart paper and tapes these to the wall. There should be one passage on each strip of paper. (People should write large enough so all group members can read the writing. The page number of the text should be written beside the passage.)

(30-45 min.)   **Present the Ideas.** One person begins by presenting one Significant Idea from the text, stating why it is significant and what implication it has for his or her work. Members of the group add to this idea after the presenter speaks. Each person has up to seven minutes to discuss this Significant Idea. This process is repeated until each person has presented a Significant Idea. If a Significant Idea is connected to another person's Significant Idea, the strips of chart paper should be moved close together. After everyone has discussed their idea and if time is available, the second set of Significant Ideas may be presented and discussed.

(3 minutes)   **Personal Write.** Participants record their ideas, connections and reflections quietly.

(3 minutes)   **Closure.** The group summarizes what they have learned together. (If there are other small groups discussing the same text these groups may report one insight to the larger group.)

(3 minutes)   **Debrief the Process.** Group members comment briefly on how the Protocol supported their learning and how they might improve upon the Protocol.

[1] The times indicated are guidelines and may be modified.

From *Classroom Assessment: What's Working in High Schools?* A. Davies and K. Busick (Eds) © Connections Publishing. May be reproduced for classroom use.

A SAMPLE PROTOCOL: LEARNING FROM SUCCESS STORIES

(From Protocols for Professional Learning Conversations, page 26)

Purpose of the Protocol:

To learn from the successes of colleagues who faced a particular challenge.

Prior to the Conversation:

The group members are given a focus for their inquiry. Examples of inquiry focus areas are: Recall a time when you successfully helped your students understand and own the expectations for high quality work. Think of a success story you have had with a student who was struggling in your class. Each group member considers the focus and prepares what he/she will share with the group. This is best done with groups of six people.

(2 minutes) **Getting Started.** Select a facilitator and a timekeeper. Review the purpose of the Protocol and ground rules for this process. The focus statement is written on the board or on chart paper.

(40 minutes) **Storytelling.** In Round Robin style moving around the circle, each person tells his/her story without interruption, for up to five minutes.

Question and Answer. After each person tells his/her story people may ask questions for two to three minutes. The timekeeper keeps the process moving.

(5 minutes) **Learnings Debriefed.** In Round Robin style, moving quickly around the circle, each person says one thing he/she learned from these stories. (If there is a larger group each small group may report one group learning.)

(Note: The times indicated are guidelines and may be modified.)

A SAMPLE PROTOCOL: FOCUSED FEEDBACK

(From page 37, Protocols for Professional Learning Conversations)

Purpose of the Protocol:

>
> To focus the feedback a presenting teacher desires from the group.

Prior to the Conversation:

>
> The presenting teacher identifies a focus question for his/her feedback session. (i.e. Is this work a good indicator of the student's ability to write persuasively? Are the criteria for this project clear? Can you see evidence that students are using the rubric to shape and improve their work?) For confidentiality and to remove potential bias, student names are removed and student work is labeled Student A, Student B, and so on. Copies of the work are made for everyone in the group. (Note: The times indicated are guidelines and may be modified.)

(2 minutes)   **Getting Started.** Select a facilitator and a timekeeper. Review the purpose of the Protocol and ground rules for this process.

(5 minutes)   **Context.** The presenting teacher offers the purpose for the assessment and any background information such as a rubric and/or criteria for the work. The focus question is written on chart paper or board for all to see.

(8 minutes)   **Review.** The group members review the student work in regard to the focus question. (If student work is lengthy, the work and the focus question may be given ahead of time.)

(10 minutes)   **Group Discussion.** Using the focus question as their guide, group members generate their insights and observation by what they see in the work. The presenting teacher is quiet.

(10 minutes)   **Dialogue.** The presenting teacher joins the discussion and directs conversation to any intriguing ideas or points to pursue.

(5 minutes)   **Reflection on the Conversation.** The group discusses how they experienced this conference and what they learned.

Resources from Connections Publishing

The following books and videos are available from Connections Publishing.
Discounts are available on bulk orders.

Classroom Assessment Resources

Making Classroom Assessment Work – Second Edition . . . . ISBN 978-0-9783193-2-8

Leading the Way to Making Classroom Assessment Work . . . . ISBN 978-0-9783139-0-4

Transforming Barriers to Assessment *for* Learning . . . . ISBN 978-0-9783193-1-1

Classroom Assessment: What's Working in High Schools?
(Two book set) . . . . ISBN 978-0-9736352-9-4

Setting and Using Criteria . . . . ISBN 978-0-9682160-1-9

Self-Assessment & Goal-Setting . . . . ISBN 978-0-9682160-2-6

Conferencing and Reporting . . . . ISBN 978-0-9682160-3-3

Assessment *of* Learning: Standards-Based Grading and Reporting
(Video Resource) . . . . ISBN 978-0-9736352-8-7

Facilitators' Resources

Protocols for Professional Learning Conversations . . . . ISBN 978-0-9682160-7-1

Facilitators' Guide to Classroom Assessment K-12 . . . . ISBN 978-0-9736352-0-1

FG Companion: Course Notes . . . . ISBN 978-0-9736352-4-9

Other Resources

Finding Proof of Learning in a One-to-One Computing Classroom
(Research Report – DVD Included) . . . . ISBN 978-0-9682160-6-4

Living Peace Series

Remember Peace . . . . ISBN 978-0-9736352-5-6

Seasons of Peace . . . . ISBN 978-0-9736352-7-0

How To Order

Phone: (800) 603-9888 (toll-free North America)
(250) 703-2920

Fax: (250) 703-2921

E-mail: books@connect2learning.com

Web: http://connect2learning.com/cp/

Post: Connections Publishing
2449D Rosewall Crescent
Courtenay, BC, V9N 8R9
Canada

Connections Publishing also sponsors events, workshops, and tele-seminars on assessment and other education-related topics, both for classroom teachers and school and district leaders. Please contact us for a full catalog.

Poems by

Jan Lee Ande

The Ashland Poetry Press
Ashland University
Ashland, Ohio 44805

Image: "Inflammation," "Redemption"
Mississippi Review: "Nothing Is What It Seems to Be"
   (previously titled "Turn of Events")
New Letters: "Hellhole Canyon"
Nimrod: "Pomegranate," "I Want to Live as a Magician"
   (previously titled "Reclaiming Land"), "Wingspun,"
   "Wounded Child," "Last Rites"
Notre Dame Review: "Poet as Oracle"
Poetry International: "The Black Arts," "What Are You
   Doing Here, García Lorca?"
Place of Passage (Story Line Press): "On Fire"
Yellow Silk: "Goethe's Theory of Color"

Printed in the United States of America

ISBN: 0-912592-46-X

Library of Congress Catalog Card Number 20-1087670

Cover art: "Walking on Water," oil on canvas, by James B. Janknegt